The STORY KEEPERS

STORIES OF JESUS KEPT ALIVE

JOHN STEPHENSON

WITH CONTRIBUTIONS FROM
LIZ HOLGATE AND ESTHER BAILEY

Scripture Union

Dedicated to Alan Wright for his example of faith and inspiration when I was a young person.

Copyright © Scripture Union 1997
First published 1997
ISBN 1 85999 197 1

Scripture Union, 207–209 Queensway,
Bletchley, Milton Keynes, MK2 2EB

This material has been published under licence from Cassell PLC. It is based on *The Storykeepers*, created by Brian Brown and Andrew Melrose. Artwork on pages 5, 22, 23, 24, 29, 31, 32, 35, 36, 38, 39, 40, 45, 47, 48, 52, 53, 55, 56, 57, 61 and 62 is taken from the series of which Jimmy Murakami was the director. Brian Brown, the Series Executive Producer, acted as a consultant in the production of this book.

The right of John Stephenson to be identified as author of this work has been asserted by him in accordance with the Copyright, Designs and Patents Act 1988.

The picture of Zacchaeus on page 23 by David Mostyn is taken from *Let's Go with Luke*, SU.

Scripture quotations are from the Contemporary English Version © American Bible Society 1991, 1992, 1995, used by permission/Anglicisations © British and Foreign Bible Society 1996.

British Library Cataloguing-in-Publication Data
A catalogue record for this book is available from the British Library.

Illustrations by Cassell and Helen Gale.
Cover design by Tony Cantale.

Printed and bound in Great Britian by Ebenezer Baylis & Son Limited, The Trinity Press, Worcester and London.

CONTENTS

The STORY KEEPERS

SETTING THE SCENE

The Storykeepers series is set in 64 AD in Rome under Nero. Along with other Roman emperors, Nero thought he was a god. Since the Christians wouldn't accept his claim and would only worship Jesus as Lord, Nero hated them. One day in Rome there was a fire and Nero blamed the Christians for starting it. He ordered his soldiers to persecute the Christians in the city. It is with this backdrop in mind that the Christians met in secret. They devised a series of signs to acknowledge each other and they sought to pass on the stories of Jesus while they faced persecution and danger from the authorities.

The parallel for us is a striking one. We have the same task as the people in the stories: we need to keep the stories of Jesus alive. Although we may not face the threat of violence and physical persecution, we live in a society where the Christian faith is only adhered to by a minority. One of the challenges we face is helping children to see that they are the storykeepers for today. They too need to hear and discover the stories of Jesus. But there is a challenge in being a storykeeper: just as the children in the story faced persecution, how are the friends of Jesus today going to face and cope with opposition?

The main characters in the stories are four children, one teenager and two adults. Three of the children – Marcus, Justin and Anna – lost their parents in the fire and so Ben the baker and Helena his wife took them into their home. Cyrus is a boy from North Africa whom they meet in the first episode. He has been separated from his family. They welcome him too. The children have adventures together and it is in the context of these adventures that the stories of Jesus are told.

USING THE CONCEPT

The concept is rich in ideas and clearly we are unable to tackle every issue using this material. The material for each episode is as follows:

- the biblical themes contained in the stories
- how they apply to the Storykeepers in the video
- applying those same themes to our lives today.

4

MEET THE HEROES

Ben the Baker is the leader of the group and is often the one who tells the stories to others at the regular meetings as well as speaking to the children informally. The Christians meet in his house and much of the preparation for these meetings is done by the children. Ben, a Jewish Christian, usually tells the stories which are in the Gospel of Mark. Mark's Gospel has a strongly Jewish flavour.

Helena is married to Ben and sometimes tells the stories to the children in an informal setting. Being a Greek Christian, she usually tells the stories from Luke's Gospel.

Zak is Ben's teenage apprentice. He likes to take charge and boss the others about. He would like to think he knows all the answers.

Justin is a fun-loving lad who is enthusiastic and keen to please.

Anna often asks questions and cares for others a lot.

Marcus is the youngest of the children, full of innocence and often comes up with the solution to the problem.

Cyrus is seen as a bit of an outsider but is accepted by the others. He is a showman who likes to be the centre of attention. He has a darker skin because he comes from North Africa – as did many of the early Christians.

There are other characters that you will meet during the video, particularly those in Nero's guard. But you'll need to watch the video to see what happens to them!! The children will easily identify with the different characters and will probably have their favourites. This can be used as a basis for conversations about the stories.

USING THIS MATERIAL

The video

The resource video that comes with this book contains five episodes. (These all come from *The Storykeepers* videos, a series of thirteen episodes available from SP Valley which you can find in your local Christian bookshop or other video outlets.) You will need a copy of the resource video to use this material. It does not stand on its own. Details of the resource video are on the inside front cover.

Each episode is a complete adventure story and contains up to three Bible stories. One twenty-five minute episode can be further divided into three acts. Details of each act are shown at the beginning of the corresponding episode in the book. In presenting the material it is suggested that in most cases you watch the three acts separately and that you finish your programme with the climax of the video in Act III.

The specific episodes have been chosen because they focus on the person of Jesus. Through them we have the chance to hear about the teaching, the miracles, the parables and the person and character of Jesus. Our aim is to introduce children to Jesus so that they can enter into a relationship with him for themselves.

The Storykeepers videos are accompanied by two series of books – one for younger readers and one for older readers. There are also activity and colouring books. These are available from Cassell. See page 64 for details.

How the ideas are arranged

In order to make the material as flexible as possible it has been presented in the format below. The sections are interdependent. There is a development from one section to another. It is important that organisers of a Storykeepers programme choose from the menu the activities which best fit their requirements and the specific needs of the children in each group. So, many suggestions and activities will need to be adapted.

BEN'S SNACK MENU

(*This material is primarily for use in a mid-week/after-school club setting.*)

This assumes you have sixty minutes available. Approximately half of this time is taken up with watching the video. There are four other elements included in the programme:

- a brief introduction to the theme for the day;
- an activity that illustrates the theme but is not directly related to the Bible content;
- a brief discussion/activity to reinforce the teaching material;
- group work which applies the lessons of the material.

There are no assumptions made about the type of room you will be using. The material aims to be as flexible as possible. However, aware of the limitations on time, the material is arranged so that the activities that come between Acts I and II are done all together. This saves time in going to and from groups.

BEN'S THREE COURSE MENU

(*This particularly relates to using the material in a holiday club setting and is based on a two-hour session.*)

There are a range of additional ideas for you to add to and develop the snack menu. For each episode a suggested programme is included for you to use the material for a holiday club. Additionally there are some specific details regarding how you would arrange your room for using the material in a holiday club setting (on page 16). Pages 11–13 have specific details to prepare the team and other leaders to make a holiday club work effectively.

STILL HUNGRY?

(*This material, generally speaking, contains ideas that will not fit into the two-hour programme and so are either ongoing projects or special events. There are ideas for adults and children, churched and non-churched.*)

At the first level of content the material is designed to focus on the person of Jesus. However we want to make the most of the parallel between the Storykeepers in the video and our role as storykeepers today. This section particularly aims to bring that home to the children.

Occasionally there is a suggestion (which is indicated) that is only appropriate for adults.

THE ACTIVITY SHEETS

There are two different sheets for each episode and they are differentiated according to age: 5–8s and 8–11s.

There is a clear progression in the activity sheets:
• The first activity reminds the storykeepers about the Bible stories they have seen and acts to reinforce the details.
• The second activity makes connections between the world of the Bible story and our world today.
• The final section helps the storykeepers to apply the Bible story to their lives today. The questions are likely to be more personal. There is also a suggestion for talking with God at the end of the activity sheet.

LET'S GET LEGAL!

The welfare of the children we are hoping to reach through The Storykeepers is of paramount importance. We are concerned for their spiritual welfare, but equally important is their physical and emotional welfare. Sadly nowadays, children are at risk more than ever before, and it is our duty to do all we can to ensure their safety and well-being as we aim to show them God's love.

As good practice, all team members need to be made aware of the current legislation arising from the Children Act 1989. The issues that affect The Storykeepers are to do with day care of children, especially relating to children under eight years, but they are appropriate for all children attending a church-run event. The following guidelines must be taken into consideration during your initial planning:

● You may need to register The Storykeepers with Social Services if you use your premises for more than two hours in a day. Any holiday club which runs for more than six days in a year must be registered, so if you are planning follow-up events, it might affect you. Phone Social Services and check with the Local Day Care Advisor – he or she is there to help!

● Requirements for accommodation state that the premises should be warm and adequately lit and ventilated. Minimum unencumbered floor space to be provided for children aged 5–8 years is 25 square feet (2.3 square metres) per child. In other words, be careful about very large numbers of children in a small hall and work out the maximum number of children who can attend.

● The premises you use will need to meet the Health and Safety requirements, so check that the owners of the premises have complied with all the requirements. Ideally there should be one toilet and one handbasin for every ten children. Disposable towels or hot-air hand driers are preferable to roller towels.

● If you are preparing food on site, you will need to be inspected by the Environmental Health Office. Ideally, any sandwiches should be refrigerated (for example, if the children bring packed lunches). No smoking should be permitted on the premises.

● Any accidents or incidents occurring during a session must be recorded in an Accident Book. This is essential in the event of any insurance claim. A record of the matter should be noted, along with details of the action taken. It should be counter-signed where appropriate.

● Everyone should be made aware of emergency procedures and fire exits and there must be access to a telephone. This could be a mobile phone, if necessary. A first-aid kit must be kept to hand and at least one member of your team should have a working knowledge of first aid.

● All groups need liability insurance. Make sure your activity is adequately covered by your church's policy.

● Recommendations for adult to child ratios are as follows:

> For 0–2 years
> – one adult to every three children (1:3)
> For 2–3 years
> – one adult to every four children (1:4)
> For 3–8 years
> – one adult to every eight children (1:8)
> For over eights
> – one adult for the first eight children, followed by one for every twelve (1:12).

● There should always be more than one adult for any group and one should be female. Let your team members know that it is not appropriate for them to talk to children alone in a secluded place – it might be misinterpreted. Do not allow people not known to you to have unsupervised access to the children. Sadly, touching children is not advisable now, although a female leader comforting a distressed young child with a cuddle would not be considered inappropriate. It is a question of common sense in this area, but if in doubt, don't!

CONFIDENTIAL DECLARATION FORM FOR POTENTIAL TEAM MEMBERS

All employed people with access to children (that is, anyone under the age of eighteen) have, by law, to make a signed declaration of any criminal record. A key recommendation in *Safe from Harm* (HMSO) also requires such a statement from volunteers. Failure to take the necessary steps could lead to a claim of negligence against the church if a child comes to any harm at the hand of anyone working with them in a voluntary capacity. 'Harm' includes ill-treatment of any kind (including sexual abuse), or impairment of physical or mental health or development.

- You should ask all potential team members to sign the form below.
- When using such a form, emphasise that it represents positive action for good practice, and slur or suspicion is not implied. Obviously the nature of the form is sensitive and should be handled with care.
- Ensure that confidentiality is maintained. In accordance with the Data Protection Act, do not divulge any information to third parties.
- If anyone gives a 'yes' answer, allow the individual to explain this disclosure personally or by letter. If you are in any doubt about the person's suitability, consult your church leader.
- As well as the declaration form, it is recommended that potential team members offer one name as a referee. Questions to ask a referee might include:

- In what capacity have you known the applicant, and for how long?
- How willing and able is he/she to work with others?
- How suitable would you consider him/her for work with children and young people?
- Are there any relevant details about this applicant which cause you concern?

CONFIDENTIAL DECLARATION

Guidelines from the Home Office following the *Children Act 1989* advise that all voluntary organisations, including churches, take steps to safeguard the children who are entrusted to their care. You are therefore asked to make the following declaration:

Have you ever been convicted of a criminal offence (including any 'spent convictions' under the Rehabilitation of Offenders Act 1974*) or been cautioned by the police or bound over to keep the peace?

☐ Yes

☐ No

Have you ever been held liable by a court for a civil wrong, or had an order made against you by a matrimonial or a family court?

☐ Yes

☐ No

Has your conduct ever caused, or been likely to cause harm to a child or put a child at risk, or, to your knowledge, has it ever been alleged that your conduct has resulted in any of these things?

☐ Yes

☐ No

Signed _____

Date _____

* Because of the nature of the work for which you are applying, this post is exempt from the provision of Section 4(ii) of the Rehabilitation of Offenders Act 1974, by virtue of the Rehabilitation of Offenders Act 1974 (Exemptions) Order 1975, and you are therefore not entitled to withhold information about convictions which, for other purposes, are 'spent' under the provisions of the Act. In the event of an appointment, any failure to disclose such convictions could result in the withdrawal of approval to work with children in the church.

WORKING WITH CHILDREN

The biblical knowledge and understanding of children has changed enormously in the last fifteen years. Whereas many adults used to have a grounding in Bible stories through Sunday school or the equivalent, nowadays society in general contains second generation non-churchgoers. This provides us with both a challenge and an opportunity.

The challenge

Children from church families may well feel marginalised in the world outside home and church. It may be easier for them to keep quiet about their faith. One of the things that *The Storykeepers* can to do is to encourage them as they seek to be open about their faith and also to help them see the importance of passing on the stories of Jesus to their friends.

Those, however, from a non-church background will come to the stories fresh and will often be excited at hearing the stories of Jesus – perhaps for the first time.

It is likely that in any group you will have a mixture of both types of children and so you will need to adapt the material accordingly, taking from Ben's snack and three course menu.

Take, for example, Episode 2 (Raging Waters).

In **BEN'S SNACK MENU**, children focus on the story of Jesus calming the storm and his amazing power. Churched children will be very familiar with this story whereas it may come as a surprise for non-churched children. Both groups will be aware of things that make them afraid and times when they need to recognise that Jesus has power.

In **BEN'S THREE COURSE MENU**, there is time to explore all of the three stories that feature in the episode. All children, at whatever stage of their faith development, can identify with the events. All can try to answer the question 'Who is Jesus?'.

STILL HUNGRY? gives scope to explore other stories of Jesus. Children may want to follow up on C5, the questionnaire option, discovering what others (adults/children/ churched and non-churched) think about Jesus.

The opportunity

Video is a highly accessible medium for children and the stories will engage them fully. They will identify easily with the characters. Although the stories may well be familiar to us, the lack of familiarity for children provides us with a real opportunity to bring the stories of Jesus alive. *The Storykeepers* presents familiar stories in a fresh way to churched children and unfamiliar stories in an accessible way to unchurched children.

Using the material with children

There are three important areas to consider when using this material with children:

The biblical content
Part of our task is to be clear in the communication of the biblical truth contained in the material. It is vital therefore that we spend time ourselves in understanding the biblical passages from which the stories are taken. In addition we should aim to engage with the Bible on every occasion of The Storykeepers. This inherently shows the source of our authority.

Building quality relationships
Children need to build relationships with adults as part of their understanding of the Christian faith. The time spent in small groups is particularly important for that, whether it is by doing a craft activity, playing a game or just chatting. Children will expect the group leader to take a lead so we must be willing to initiate conversations. If we want children to talk about things in their lives, we need to be willing to share our lives with them. Always be ready to illustrate the things you talk about with stories from your own life that help the children to see that you practise what you preach!

Demonstrating Christian living
It is not only our words but our lives that speak to children about Christian truth. Take care to show attitudes of justice and honesty in dealings with the children. This is particularly important when playing a game or running a quiz. Everything we do must show that we belong to Jesus and that he is in control of our lives. Our overriding attitude needs to be that of servanthood. The children need to be able to see Jesus in us. Remember that for some storykeepers, you may be the first (or the only) Christian they know.

For more information about each of these areas see *Reaching Children*, Paul Butler (SU).

Children and faith development

The prime purpose of this resource book is for children to be introduced to Jesus through *The Storykeepers*. This may be a first introduction for some and for others it will be strengthening their existing faith. It is very easy to adopt an approach to evangelism which centres on a once-and-for-all decision. It is more helpful to think of faith as a journey. On this journey each child makes significant steps of faith. Our aim is that every child involved in The Storykeepers will move forward in their journey of faith. As part of that it is appropriate to offer children the opportunity to make a response and to indicate this in an appropriate way.

In thinking about the responses that children make it is important to bear in mind:

1 The developmental stage of the child

Children under the age of eleven still largely think in concrete terms and interpret things literally. This means that the language we use needs to be appropriate to them. Beginning a relationship with Jesus should be talked about in terms of 'becoming a friend of Jesus' rather than 'opening the door of our lives/hearts'. Remember that children of this age are keen to please those from whom they wish to have approval. They may want to respond to us rather than to God. We need to offer the chance to respond in a non-pressured way that respects the integrity of children.

2 The faith stage of the child

Faith in children of this age is largely of two types:
Experienced faith
They see and experience something in the adults around them and this becomes part of their experience of faith. For many children their understanding of concepts such as love, security, acceptance, forgiveness, trust and self-esteem may have already been damaged by their experience with others. A leader's task is to rebuild those ideas through relationships with them – these ideas are integral to a child's concept of God and so to their faith development. The way they are treated is key to this aspect of faith.

Affiliative faith
This stage of faith development builds on experienced faith and is largely to do with belonging. Children see an example of faith that they want to emulate. They want that to be part of their lives and so they affiliate to the faith of the people around them. (Affiliative faith is about belonging.) Giving them a sense that they belong to The Storykeepers is really important. We need to help them see they can also belong to God. This is an important stage in their faith journey and for many children The Storykeepers will provide the opportunity for that to take place.

Children need to have their faith taken seriously. They may not always express their ideas with theological correctness! What is important is that their expressions of faith are taken seriously and that they are given opportunities to move forward in their faith.

As children enter adolescence, they begin to ask questions about faith. This stage of faith development – searching faith – is to be expected.

The role of adults in faith development

Adults play two distinctive roles in relation to faith development:

• Faith advocates. In this role the task is to bring children into situations where they see faith as attractive. This is achieved in two main ways: a) by being near to faith and its practices and b) by using specific occasions of direct challenge. This needs to be done in a way that respects the integrity of children and enables them to respond freely.
• Faith clarifiers. In this role the task is to help young people clarify questions about faith. The work that we do in small groups is a particularly significant way of achieving this task.

Praying with children

As part of each session children can be encouraged to learn about prayer. Giving time for children to write down a prayer and then read it out loud may be a valuable way of including all children, not just the articulate. We need to introduce prayer as talking to God and help children to be natural in the way that they express it. When we pray, we need to use words that are familiar to their vocabulary too.

We must respect the integrity of children in prayer. Rather than saying 'Let us pray', we may invite the children to pray but make clear to them that they don't have to pray if they don't want to. Never pressurise children to pray, just encourage. You will be surprised at how naturally children can pray about things – often things that we as adults think are too trivial for God to deal with. Children have lots to teach adults! For more ideas see *101 Creative ways to pray*, Judith Merrell (SU).

USING THE MATERIAL IN A HOLIDAY CLUB SETTING

BEFORE THE HOLIDAY CLUB

Getting the team together

You cannot run The Storykeepers holiday club on your own. You will need a team of people. Within this team there will be people with differing gifts: some who are good at speaking, a musician or two, a technical person, some to help with things like registration and refreshments. Make sure you have everyone you need and spend some time together in advance both for preparation and prayer. Ideally, set aside a full day at least two weeks before The Storykeepers to make sure everyone knows what is required of them. Try out all the practical ideas.

As part of good practice you need to give some training to your team members before the event. Topics that are vital to cover are safety, dealing with problems and the Children Act, as well as practical issues regarding the procedures for registration and contact with parents. Make sure that all those who are helping with The Storykeepers have completed a Confidential Declaration Form in advance. See page 8.

Publicity and consent forms

Make sure your publicity is eye-catching. Use *The Storykeepers* logo and characters on your posters or on the reverse of the initial registration form.

There is increasing concern about the access that adults have to children. As well as acting wisely with regard to team members, we need to be sure that parents are aware of what children are coming too. This means any publicity sent out in advance needs to clearly state the nature of the activity. On page 63 there is a sample letter to parents with a registration form.

Further information and consent form

Once a child has registered for The Storykeepers more information is needed about them. This information needs to be returned to the coordinator and kept at the venue. It should include the following:

Name, address, phone number and age of the child
Emergency contact telephone number
GP's name and telephone number
Details of any known conditions or allergies
Name of the person collecting the child at the end of The Storykeepers

In the unlikely event of illness or accident I give permission for any necessary medical treatment to be given by the nominated first aider. In an emergency and if I am not contactable, I am willing for my son/daughter to receive hospital treatment, including an anaesthetic. I understand that every effort will be made to contact me as soon as possible.

I confirm that the above details are correct to the best of my knowledge.

Signed . . . . Parent/Guardian

Date . . . .

Venue

Check the venue in advance. Make sure that you are aware of all fire exits and extinguishers. Make notices for directions to the toilets and check the suitability of all rooms. You should have a first aider present and they should check the first-aid kit and place it in a safe but easily accessible place. Collect together all the equipment you will need and make sure that the rooms are set out in plenty of time before the children arrive. A suggested layout for the venue is given on page 16. This will mean that the team needs to arrive about one hour before the children every day. Where possible try to arrange to have the venue all week so that you can leave some items in place. This will save considerable time every day.

Equipment

For each day look at the 'You will need' section. A TV and video player is needed for everyday.

Dos and don'ts for using a video.

- DO check all your equipment before you start.

- DO make sure every storykeeper can see a screen. Once the group size exceeds thirty you will need to run two TV's from one video using a splitter. In order to make a real impact *The Storykeepers* video can be shown using a modern video projector. These are available for hire from local Audio Visual firms. Although they are expensive it is well worth it as this part of the programme forms a key part of your teaching input.

- DO check the volume of the video recorder. You are likely to need some form of PA equipment as the speakers on a video projector are too small for a large group.

- DO make sure the room is dark enough. If you are using a darkened area in The Catacombs each session, make sure it is clear where groups are to sit. Control the movement of storykeepers carefully.

- DO run through each episode beforehand so that you know when to stop each section. It is worth timing these so you know how long each section takes. There is no clear indication on the video when the break comes.

- DO make sure any children with disabilities are catered for.

- DON'T just see the video as a useful filler for 25 minutes!

- DON'T leave the storykeepers to watch the video unattended. Encourage group leaders to sit with their group.

- DO appoint a leader as the video operator. Lots of storykeepers will offer advice, but may not have the required expertise!

Don't forget to order copies of *The Storykeepers* books (see inside back cover) and The Storykeepers merchandise. Badges for the children and t-shirts for leaders are available. See the inside front cover for details.

DURING THE HOLIDAY CLUB

For each episode there is a programme entitled **BEN'S THREE COURSE MENU**. This is a two hour programme with detailed timings. Throughout this programme the children are called storykeepers. You should do the same to help them identify closely with the theme. The format for each episode is basically the same:

INTRODUCTORY ACTIVITY

This will involve making something as the children arrive. It provides an opportunity to get to know each other and to check the register. On each day the item they make becomes the entry permit they need to gain access to The Catacombs for the video and meeting part of the morning.

SECRET MEETING – PART 1

The first part of the morning happens in The Catacombs. This will normally involve watching Act I on video, singing the *Keep the story alive* song and an activity to stimulate the children into thinking about the issues.

MARKET PLACE

On each day set out the various activities like market stalls. Storykeepers can then try out different stalls. In some cases they will spend all their time at one stall; in others they will try three or four things.

REFRESHMENTS

Don't underestimate the importance of this slot as a natural break from the busyness of the morning.

SECRET MEETING – PART 2

Back in the Catacombs you will watch Act II, sing the song again and there will normally be a discussion about the significance of the Bible stories.

GROUP WORK

This is a vital part of the programme for relationship-building and is also the time for applying the meaning of the Bible stories to our lives.

SECRET MEETING – PART 3

This will be very short – normally five minutes maximum. This is the climax to the story on the video and children will look forward to finding out what happens.

AFTER THE HOLIDAY CLUB

Details for follow-up events are contained in **STILL HUNGRY?**. There are also details of how to organise an event for parents on page 59. Encourage team leaders to maintain appropriate contact with storykeepers in their group.

One of the best ways to follow up The Storykeepers holiday club is with a regular Storykeepers club, meeting weekly after school. You could then use some of the ideas you haven't used in this resource book. There are another eight episodes of video as an untapped resource. Remember that because of the richness of the material you could come back to the same video and take a different approach or focus on one of the other featured Bible stories.

Keep the story alive

Gill Hutchinson

We've been told a story,
The best there will ever be,
About Jesus and the things he did,
About his love for you and me.
We think it's amazing,
And everyone really tries
To keep the story spreading round,
So that the good news never dies.
And so we'll tell the story, pass it on,
Spread the news to everyone,
Keep the story alive,
So the news of Jesus will survive for ever,
Pass it on so people hear,
Tell the story, make it clear,
So the news of Jesus will survive,
Keep the story alive.
Keep the story alive.

You will need to create space for small groups to meet – either by rearranging the market place or by using other rooms. Some of the suggested games need space as well!

The Catacombs

Video projector, OHP screen. Low lighting and carpet on the floor. Rocks or boulders and netting to lower the ceiling would increase the underground atmosphere.

windows blacked out

Café

for refreshments.

The market place

Stalls laid out for craft activities.

Coloured awning and bright tablecloths would create a busy outdoor scene.

A wheelbarrow could become a bread stall.

Welcome and opening activities in small groups.

Registration

EPISODE 1

BREAKOUT!

. . . .

AIM

To show that hearing the stories of Jesus and meeting him can be a life-changing experience.

THE STORY IN BRIEF

ACT I

Ben, the baker, distributes bread through the bazaar, accompanied by his wife Helena, Anna, Marcus and Zak. They also spread word about the secret meeting of the Christians that evening. Anna invites Cyrus, a child juggler, to the meeting, even though he is a stranger. This makes Zak cross. The Christians enter the meeting place with a secret knock and by giving the 'Ichthus' fish sign. Cyrus watches this, hidden in a barrel. Ben begins his story, but is interrupted by Cyrus' arrival. Ben continues to talk about Jesus' command to love and pray for our enemies followed by **The feeding of the 5000**. There is a pounding on the door – Roman soldiers! Zak thinks Cyrus has betrayed them. Everyone hides. There is a commotion, many escape, but Cyrus is arrested.

ACT II

Nero is imagining tomorrow's games: Giganticus in the arena. He has a scale model of it. He needs Christians as victims for Giganticus. Nihilus promises to provide some. Anna and Helena search for Cyrus' parents. They discover he's a homeless orphan. They decide to rescue him from prison. Zak makes a map of the prison while Ben and the others find Cyrus with other Christians. The prisoners are frightened but Ben encourages them to be courageous, and tells them **The story of Zacchaeus** who was courageous enough to do the right thing. They return to the bakery where they make a skeleton key to the prison and a copy of the map. They talk about the power of Giganticus. But **The story of Jesus healing Jairus' daughter** encourages them that Jesus is more powerful.

ACT III

In the arena, Giganticus demonstrates his strength. The Christians escape from their prison cell, but Zak accidentally leads them into the arena. By his juggling, Cyrus distracts Giganticus and helps them all to escape just in time. That evening, they invite Cyrus to live with them.

BIBLE BASE

The stories in this episode of *The Storykeepers* can be found in the following passages:

Story One	Feeding the 5,000	Mark 6:30–44	told by Ben
Story Two	Zacchaeus	Luke 19:1–10	told by Helena
Story Three	Jairus' daughter	Mark 5:21–43	told by Ben

BEN'S SNACK MENU
(60 MINS)

5 mins	**A1**	Introduction
11 mins	**A2**	Video: Act I
5 mins	**A3**	Question/answer quiz
4 mins	**A4**	*Keep the story alive* song
10 mins	**A5**	Video: Act II
10 mins	**A6**	Find the treasure
10 mins	**A7**	Group work
6 mins	**A8**	Video: Act III

RECOMMENDED BEN'S THREE COURSE MENU
(2 HOURS)

10.00	**B1**	Badge making and **B2** Puzzles (welcoming activities)
10.10	**A1**, **A2**	(Video: Act I) and **A4**
10.35	**B4**	Craft activities *or* **B5** Team games
10.55		Refreshments
11.05	**A5**	(Video: Act II) and **A6**
11.25	**B6**	Group work
11.45	**A8**	(Video: Act III)

YOU WILL NEED

- *The Storykeepers* video
- Words of *Keep the story alive* song on acetate plus an overhead projector

A1: Clothes for dressing up Roman characters and the map of the Roman Empire (page 58).

A3: Several large cards numbered 1, 2 and 3 for the run around quiz.

A3: A large foam dice or string and a saucepan with a lid for the question/answer quiz.

A6: Copies of the following message from the story of Zacchaeus:

> 'Once Zacchaeus/had met/Jesus/he wanted/to stop/being/a/cheat.'

Cut up the messsage into eight pieces to make one jigsaw. You will need enough for each group of storykeepers to have a set of pieces. You could use a different colour for each group.

A7: 5–8s One packed lunch box (full!).
8–11s Large sheets of paper for making the front page of a newspaper.

B1: Card, safety pins and sellotape to make fish badges or enough Storykeeper badges (available from Scripture Union – see front cover for details).

B2: Mazes, number puzzles, chocolate, assorted locks, 'treasure chests', pictures of characters (see page 57) stuck on card for a simple game of snap, 'dotty' pictures, Roman numeral sums.

B3: An enlarged map of the locality, coloured dots, squared paper.

B4: Air drying clay, *Fimo*, *Soff-Mo*.

B5: Scrap material, balloons, newspapers, buckets, foam ball.

B6: One copy of the activity sheet for each child. (For the 8s–11s you will need a response box and scissors.)

BEN'S SNACK MENU

A1: INTRODUCTION (5 MINS)

Since this is the first episode of the video it is essential to put the whole series in its broader context by giving an explanation of the Roman background. Do this with the help of three dressed-up characters to introduce the key ideas. A map of the Roman empire on page 58 is a valuable prop.

NARRATOR: dressed in a toga (a sheet will do) with a grand purple sash. He explains what Rome is like.

NERO: dressed as the emperor (a leaf headband or wreath would be effective). He introduces himself and talks about being a god. These Christians are troublemakers. The cartoon Nero provides the model.

SOLDIER: in a tunic with a sword, talks about life as a soldier.

Narrator: Hello and welcome to Rome. Here it is on the map. It is 64 AD and I am here to let you know what is happening in our great city. We are the centre of the Roman empire which spreads over most of Europe – look at the area it covers. We have the best houses, the best army, the best food and the best entertainment in the whole world right here in our city! Of course we have the best emperor in the whole world too. Here he comes now.

Nero: My name is Nero. I am the ruler of the Roman empire and I am truly great and amazing – there is no one as great as I am. In fact I am so great that people worship me as a god, and quite right too – I am a god. I am the most powerful man in the whole world – everything around me is mine. People will do as I say or else. I am a wonderful singer, as you will find out, and people adore me because of my singing. But I have one big problem. There's this group of troublemakers in Rome – Christians, they call themselves. But I'll soon put a stop to them with the help of my army, the strongest army in the world. 'Guards!'

Soldier: Life in the Roman army is tough, but that's what you'd expect. The Roman army is the toughest army – that's why we win so many battles. We are here to do the will of the emperor. We have to keep order in Rome. Nobody moves or even breathes without agreement. Roman soldiers are feared as fighting men. If there's any trouble we will sort it out, no fear. Just you watch out. We'll sort you out too if you cause any trouble!

Narrator: So that's it. You'd better watch out. But come to Rome – there's no place better in the whole Roman empire. It's a good life, just so long as you keep on the right side of the army and the emperor.

A2: VIDEO: ACT I (11 MINS)

End after Cyrus is taken away and before the scene with Nero in his throne room.

A3: QUIZ (5 MINS)

In order to follow the stories it is vital that the storykeepers gain a clear understanding of the main characters in the video. Each of them had the responsibility of keeping alive the stories of Jesus which had not yet been written down. At great personal risk, they passed on the stories by word of mouth. Today's storykeepers need to understand that just as Ben and the others had the job of keeping the stories of Jesus alive in their day, so we have the job of doing the same today. Most of the characters appear in this first act so a quiz will help to reinforce the details. The key biographical details are as follows:

BEN	Baker, Jewish, Storykeeper
HELENA	Baker, Ben's wife, Greek
ZAK	Christian, Ben's apprentice
ANNA, MARCUS and JUSTIN	Lost their parents in the fire in Rome. Live with Ben and Helena
CYRUS	Juggler who is separated from his parents

Watch the first part of the video to prepare a list of appropriate questions and then run one of the following quizzes:

Run around quiz

Make three cards numbered 1, 2 and 3. Place them in three corners of your meeting room. After each question, read out three numbered possible answers – storykeepers have to run to the number that they think is the correct answer.

Question/answer quiz

For each correct answer the team can roll the dice. The winning team is the one with the highest score. Alternatively cut up different lengths of string. Place them in a saucepan with equal lengths of string on display. Put the lid on.

For each correct answer a storykeeper chooses a length of string. The winning team is the one with the longest total length of string tied together.

NB Children get very excited by quizzes so keep firm control.

For extra quiz ideas see *Quiz Resource Book*, Richard and Mary Chewter (SU) or *Pick N' Mix*, Judith Merrell (SU).

A4: SONG (5 MINS)
Teach the *Keep the story alive* song on page 14.

A5: VIDEO: ACT II (10 MINS)
End as Ben tucks the children up in bed.

A6: FIND THE TREASURE (10 MINS)
Around the room hide the jigsaw pieces of the message from the Zacchaeus story. Don't make it too difficult. Make sure you have enough sets of this verse for each group of storykeepers.

Explain that a message from one of the stories of Jesus has been hidden like treasure around the room. Storykeepers have to find the pieces and put them together to work out the message. These stories about Jesus are real events. They are stories about people whose lives changed when they met Jesus. As we learn the stories about Jesus and meet him today, our lives too will be changed.

A7: GROUP WORK (10 MINS.)
5–8s: Bring one packed lunch with you and share it among the group – is anyone full? Jesus was able to help 5,000 people. He wants to help us too. In what ways do we want him to help us? End by praying for the things the children mention and ask Jesus to help. You may be able to follow this up on another occasion.
8–11s: Try to design the front page of a newspaper which tells the story of Zacchaeus. Storykeepers will need a title for the paper, a headline, a 'photo' and details of the story. Use this to discuss the ways that Zacchaeus changed. In what ways might God want us to behave differently?

A8: VIDEO ACT: III (6 MINS)

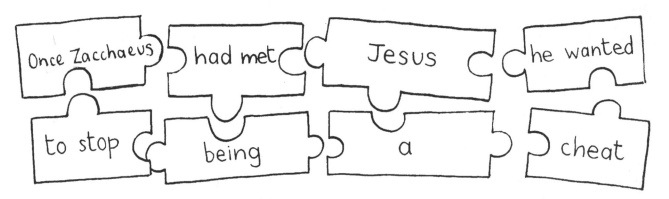

BEN'S THREE COURSE MENU

It is essential that group leaders are ready to welcome storykeepers on the first day. Both B1 and B2 are designed to keep the children busy in an environment where they can introduce themselves and begin the process of relationship-building.

B1: BADGE MAKING (10 MINS)
Storykeeper badges with the fish sign and space for a child's name are available from Scripture Union (see the inside front cover for details). Alternatively prepare some card badges in the shape of a fish with stiff card, safety pins and sellotape. Storykeepers can write their name on the badge and colour it.

The badge is today's entry permit into The Catacombs.

B2: PUZZLES (10 MINS)
Lay out some of the following, depending upon space available.
● A series of mazes for storykeepers to solve. There are a number on the market, some of which are quite complex.
● Number puzzles which involve cracking a combination, eg opening a safe or unlocking a treasure chest. In order to make this more fun you could have a series of items chained or locked up with a combination lock with a mini-bar of chocolate inside, eg a briefcase, bicycle chain,

combination lock on a box.

● Pictures of Ben and the other Storykeeper characters on page 57, stuck on card for a simple game of snap.

● Pictures with some shapes containing a dot. Only the dotted shapes are to be coloured. These could spell a word or a simple picture based on *The Storykeepers*.

● For older storykeepers interested in numbers, introduce Roman numerals and write out some sums to solve. They can then write their own sums too.

B3: MAPS (5–10 MINS)

● Photocopy an enlarged map of the local area. Storykeepers put a coloured dot where they live and see what pattern develops.

● Co-ordinates can be great fun especially for older storykeepers. Explain how they work and then give each storykeeper some squared paper and the reference points. When they have joined up the points, they can shade in the shape. See an example below. You can no doubt think of other shapes. Remember, always start with the point on the horizontal line. This links with Act II of the video.

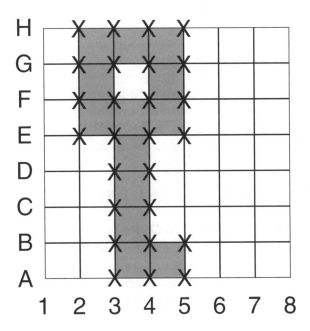

Outside
3A; 3B; 3C; 3D; 3E; 2E; 2F; 2G; 2H; 3H; 4H; 5H; 5G; 5F; 5E; 4E; 4D; 4C; 4B; 5B; 5A; 4A.
Inside
3F; 3G; 4G; 4F.

B4: CRAFT ACTIVITIES (20 MINS)

● Clay pots. Use some air drying clay (*Newclay*) to make small pots. This is a really messy activity but everyone can have a go. Storykeepers should wear an old shirt and cover all work surfaces!

● Invite someone to come to demonstrate a potter's wheel.

● *Fimo* badges. Storykeepers make colourful fish badges out of *Fimo* or *Soff-Mo* and bake in the oven to take home at the end of the session. This duplicates **B1**.

B5: TEAM GAMES (20 MINS)

● Bring lots of cardboard boxes, coloured paper and general scrap. Each team of storykeepers tries to dress up a team member as a Roman soldier using the scrap. All those brave enough to take part deserve a prize!

● Since the arena in Rome was a place for competition, play some team games involving two large teams. All storykeepers line up in height order and are numbered alternatively. This will mean that in the games below the two teams are fairly equal. Two suggestions for games are:

a) **Balloon Hockey**. You will need two buckets, two rolled-up newspapers (sellotaped to make a stick) and plenty of balloons. Teams sit opposite each other and are numbered like this:

1 2 3 4 5 6 7 8 9

Team A		Team B
Bucket	Balloon	Bucket

9 8 7 6 5 4 3 2 1

To score a point a team has to place a balloon in their bucket using the newspaper stick. Call out a number and the two storykeepers with this number try to hit the balloon into their bucket. Change over when a point is scored or after forty-five seconds. Make sure everyone gets a go.

b) **Human netball**. The 'basket' is provided by the arms of two people standing at either end of the hall on a plastic box or a low table. Use a foam ball – no contact, just passing. A point is scored every time a clean catch is made by the basket.

B6: GROUP WORK/ACTIVITY SHEETS (20 MINS)

Some children may be afraid to share secrets. Others will remember that they are encouraged to confide in an adult they trust, which is what you may become during The Storykeepers. Remind yourself of the confidentiality issues on page 8.

Meeting in secret was the only way to be safe and keep the stories of Jesus alive, so we had to have a secret sign. Can storykeepers remember what it is? Storykeepers of both age groups explore the fish sign.

Jesus was very powerful but he used his power to help others. With both age groups talk about the people Jesus helped in the stories, how and why. In what ways can he help storykeepers today?

Jesus wants to help us today.

Be realistic and practical, identifying how he can help today. In thinking of the story of Zacchaeus, storykeepers will realise that Jesus helped Zacchaeus to change and turn his back on his life of cheating.

With the older children especially, explore ways in which children may want to change in their behaviour and attitudes, if these are things which displease God. Note that some children may want to be taller, a genius, better at sports. This provides an opportunity to make the distinction between accepting ourselves as God has made us but seeing self-centred behaviour as being sin in God's eyes. Encourage the storykeepers to write down their thoughts and comments to God.

8–11s: On the activity sheet there is a corner for storykeepers to write down what they want to change. Encourage them to cut out the corner and put it in a response box. Do stress that this is done anonymously.

STILL HUNGRY?

C1: SYMBOLS

There are other symbols apart from the fish sign that the early Christians used. They were a way of letting others know about their faith too. One of the most famous is the sator square. You can find details of this in *Drawing on the Past* published by Eagle, p12–14. The whole of the first section deals with Christianity in the Roman era. What symbols might we use today to explain our faith in Jesus to others?

C2: BANNER MAKING

Bring in some banners from the church as examples if you have them. Ask the storykeepers to think about which design would suit a Storykeepers banner. As a group, work on producing a banner which explains the task of keeping the stories of Jesus alive today. For further details about banners see *Here's one I made earlier*, Kathryn Copsey (SU).

C3: TREASURE HUNT

For a special event you could organise an afternoon or an early evening treasure hunt. Use

a limited part of your locality and pin clues to railings, trees, shop windows (with permission!). Each clue provides the directions to the next one and a letter for them to solve a puzzle at the end. Do the treasure hunt in groups of five or six with an adult and arrange a pre-determined time to be back at your venue. Buy some chocolate coins as treasure for all participants.

FOR ADULTS AND CHILDREN

C5: READ MARK'S GOSPEL

The Storykeepers is based upon Mark's Gospel, although some of the stories are found in other Gospels. Using drama, song, dramatic reading, dance and video, work out how you can cover the whole gospel. You could present this as a special event on, for example, Good Friday. This can involve all ages.

C6: CLAY MODELLING

As in **B4**, use clay to create a shape that symbolises one of the three stories in this episode of *The Storykeepers*.

BREAKOUT!

Can you think of at least two people Jesus helped in today's stories?

Can you finish off this picture of one of them?

The Christians used a secret sign. Draw it in the space below.

SECRET SIGN

Jesus wants to help us today. He knows what we need. Draw a picture of someone you want Jesus to help.

Talk to God by completing this prayer:

Dear God, please help me

to _____

and help _____ because

_____ Amen.

BREAKOUT!

The Christians used a secret sign to show that they were followers of Jesus.

There are times when we feel left out. Tick the boxes for the times you have felt like that.

Each letter stands for a word in Greek. (The stories of Jesus were first written down in Greek.) Work out the words in English by taking the first letter of each of these pictures.

- [ ] The smallest person
- [ ] In a crowd of people – football, squashed on a bus
- [ ] In the playground at school
- [ ] Moving house
- [ ] Being bullied
- [ ] Other _____

Which people did Jesus help in today's stories? How did they feel when he helped them?

_____

— — — — —   — — —

— — —   — — — — —

Talk to God and ask him to help you when you feel left out.

— — — — — — —

Once Zacchaeus had met Jesus he wanted to stop being a cheat.

Cut out this corner and put it in the response box.

How *might* Jesus want you to behave *differently* if you are doing things, like Zacchaeus, which do *not* please him?
Write it here.

EPISODE 2

RAGING WATERS

· · · · · · · · · · · · ·

AIM

To give a sense of wonder at who Jesus is and what he has done.

THE STORY IN BRIEF

ACT I

Zak is being chased by Roman soldiers. He escapes to Ben's house where he announces that the Storykeeper in the north of the city has been captured. Ben can't go there to tell the story as he is speaking at another meeting. He plans to tell **The story of John the Baptist** and **Jesus' baptism**. They hide a story written on a scroll in some bread. The children are sent to deliver it in the north by travelling on a barrel through the aqueducts, but they end up in a water filter station where a soldier, biting into the bread, discovers the scroll. Zak is arrested.

ACT II

Ben cooks up a plan to rescue Zak. Nero is singing in his palace, when Zak is brought before him. Nero commands Zak to read the story on the scroll found in the bread roll, but Zak refuses. He doesn't want Jesus mocked. Instead a soldier, Tacticus, reads **The story about Jesus calming the storm**. The people are captivated. At the end of the story Nero is annoyed. He orders Zak to be thrown to the lions the next day. Meanwhile Ben is waiting to deliver his cakes to Nero. The family talk about Nero's madness which leads to **The story of Jesus healing the wild man**.

ACT III

Ben and Helena and the gang arrive at Nero's palace dressed as Gallic bakers. They tempt Nero with pastries and then produce a 'poisoned' cake. Nero tries out a 'poisoned' cake on Zak who pretends to die. But as he escapes Zak sneezes. The chase is on. They all escape via the aqueducts and finally arrive in the north of the city where they throw down the scroll to the waiting Christians. The episode closes with another reading of **The story of the calming of the storm**.

BIBLE BASE

The stories in this episode of *The Storykeepers* can be found in the following passages:

Story One	John the Baptist; Jesus' baptism	Mark 1:1–11	told by Ben
Story Two	Calming the storm	Mark 4:35–41	read by Tacticus from the scroll
Story Three	The wild man	Mark 5:1–20	told by Ben

BEN'S SNACK MENU
(60 MINS)

5 mins	**A1**	Song
12 mins	**A2**	Video: Act I
5 mins	**A3**	Codebreaders
5 mins	**A4**	Sign language
10 mins	**A5**	Video: Act II
5 mins	**A6**	Demonstration
10 mins	**A7**	Group work
5 mins	**A8**	Video: Act III

RECOMMENDED BEN'S THREE COURSE MENU
(2 HOURS)

10.00	**B1**	Making scrolls
10.10	**A1** and **A2** (Video: Act 1)
10.25	**A3**, **A4**, **A5** or **B2**
10.40	**B3**	Refreshments
10.50	**A6** (Video: Act II) and **A7**
11.10	**B4** Bakery or **B5** Invitations
11.30	**B6**	Group work
11.50	**A9** (Video: Act III), and decoding the messages.

YOU WILL NEED

- *The Storykeepers* video
- Acetate words of the *Keep the story alive* song plus an overhead projector
- Two secret messages are used in this episode.

Message 1 (see **B1**) is   'JESUS, SON OF THE MOST HIGH GOD.'

Message 2 (see **A6**, **B4**) is   'GUESS WHAT? JESUS HAS POWER OVER A POWERFUL STORM!'

A3: Display a code (such as the Wingdings font in Microsoft Word shown below) on an acetate or large sheet of   paper. You may want to use a number of codes. Ideas are given below:

a   b   c   d   e   f   g   h   i   j   k   l   m   n   o   p   q   r   s   t   u   v   w   x   y   z

- A=1, B=2, etc.

NB With younger children it is better to put only a few letters in code, eg

     s = ♦   e = ♏   Jesus = J♏♦u♦

A4: Someone to demonstrate sign language.

A6: For the demonstration, a part-baked baguette and rice paper, or ingredients for making bread. You will need to find a bread recipe in a cookery book. The secret message needs to written on rice paper or baking paper. You will need a codebreaker. You may want to enlarge the illustrations on the activity sheet on page 31 to remind storykeepers of the stories.

A7: 5–8s Pens and paper for drawing faces or expressionless faces, already drawn, for completion. 8–11s Large sheets of paper, old magazines and newspapers for pictures and headlines, scissors and glue. Paper people shapes.

B1: Wooden dowel or toilet roll/kitchen towel holders, lining paper cut into equal lengths, tea and candles for aging the paper, felt-tip pens – brown or metallic would be good. Codes plus codebreaker from **A3** for secret message 1.

B2 : Code sheets, colour changing pens, string and large yoghurt pots, helium cylinder, balloons and parcel labels.

B3 : Buns baked with food colouring inside.

B4 : Bread dough prepared in advance. A code plus codebreaker for secret message 2.

B5 : Pens, paper or card and artwork for invitations.

B6 : One copy of the activity sheet for each child.

BEN'S SNACK MENU

A1: SINGING (5 MINS)
Remind the storykeepers what it was like to meet in secret and then sing a song that talks about Jesus. Reintroduce the *Keep the story alive* song.

A2: VIDEO: ACT I (12 MINS)
End as Zak is arrested. This reminds the children of *The Storykeepers* setting and introduces the main storyline and the first story about Jesus' baptism in the river Jordan. After the video, talk briefly about the idea of communication. Before Jesus came, God spoke to his people through prophets who passed on God's message. When Jesus came people weren't sure who he was. Here we get the first hint of who Jesus is. It was only gradually, during Jesus' life and ministry, that some people began to understand. This is a key point in Mark's Gospel.

A3: CODEBREAKERS (5 MINS)
Introduce the simple code on the acetate or large sheet of paper. Ask storykeepers to write their names or simple messages to one another.

A4: SIGN LANGUAGE (5 MINS)
Ask someone to come and demonstrate sign language.

A5: VIDEO: ACT II (10 MINS)
End as the rescuers arrive at the palace. This contains the main teaching content of the day. Remind the children that the question everyone was asking was 'Who is Jesus?'. Remind them also of the situation that Ben and the children are in.

A6: DEMONSTRATION (5 MINS)
The day before, you need to prepare a loaf of bread with the coded message 2 inside it. You can do this in two ways:

• Use a split part-baked baguette. Write the secret message on rice/baking paper, place inside and cook the baguette.

• Bake a loaf using the recipe from a cookery book. Fold the bread around the rice paper with the secret message and bake in the oven.

Check that the storykeepers have understood the three stories. You may want to use enlarged illustrations from the activity sheet on page 31. Remind them that after calming the storm and restoring the wild man, people were amazed and asked, 'Who is this man, Jesus?' and pose the question again, 'Who is Jesus?' Each of the three stories give us hints of the answer to that question. What does each story show us about who Jesus is? Write down the storykeepers' answers on an acetate or large sheet of paper.

Produce the loaf and give it to some storykeepers to break open. When they have found the secret message, ask the children to crack the code, using the appropriate codebreaker. Encourage storykeepers to recognise the amazing nature of what Jesus had done.

A7 : GROUP WORK (10 MINS)

5–8s: Encourage the children to think about the story of Jesus calming the storm. Imagine they were one of the disciples. Get them to draw a face to show how they might have felt when the storm started. Now draw another face to show how you would have felt when the storm stopped. You could draw some expressionless faces for the children to complete the expression or have a face on a paper plate, drawn in such a way that one way up it is happy, the other way up it is sad. Talk about the things that make children afraid and ask Jesus to be with us at such times. He can make a difference.

8–11s: In the stories Jesus showed his amazing power. This activity is to help storykeepers think about the things in their own life or in the world around that need to change. (It follows on from the story of Zacchaeus.)

Cut out pictures or headlines from newspapers of the things that are wrong in the world and need to change. Stick them on to a large sheet of paper. Jesus is able to do something about the wrong in the world. Talk to God thanking him that Jesus is more powerful than all these things. Ask him to change what is wrong. Is there anything that storykeepers can also do to help Jesus bring about change?

A8: VIDEO: ACT III (5 MINS)

BEN'S THREE COURSE MENU

B1: SCROLL MAKING (10 MINS)

The task is to make scrolls from the dowels and the papers. Without understanding it, the storykeepers can write secret message 1 on the scroll in code, using one of the codes in **A3**. These are the words the wild man said when he first saw Jesus. Paper can be aged by soaking it in cold tea and then dried. You could carefully burn the edges with a candle or match. For safety reasons you ought to do this task in advance! Use sellotape to attach the paper to the dowel/holder to make a scroll.

The final activity of your session should be to decipher the code once the storykeepers know the codebreaker. This provides a further opportunity to talk about the power of Jesus.

This is today's entry permit to The Catacombs. Group leaders may need to look after the permits until the storykeepers need them. Make sure each scroll is named correctly.

B2: COMMUNICATIONS (15 MINS)

Choose from the following:

● **Codes:** provide a range of code sheets and messages for storykeepers to solve. Storykeepers can write coded messages to each other as well. Examples of codes you could use are given in **A3**.

● **Invisible writing:** there are a range of colour-changing pens on the market to draw on paper in 'invisible ink'.

● **String telephones:** prepare the materials for making these from large yoghurt pots and string. Punch the holes in advance. Storykeepers can thread and tie the strings and can then talk to each other.

● **Helium balloons:** using a helium cylinder, fill the balloons. Tie long strings to them with a card attached. Storykeepers can write their names on one side of the card. Prepare the other side of the card with the address of the venue and a request to write back when the balloon is found.

B3: REFRESHMENTS (10 MINS)

Instead of biscuits, prepare some cakes or buns with food colouring in the middle. They will serve as a talking point after the last section of the video when Ben has offered Nero his 'poisoned cakes'.

B4: BREAD-MAKING (10 MINS)

Prepare the bread dough using a recipe from a recipe book. Write secret message 2 on small pieces of rice paper and place the message inside. Knead the dough into different shapes. Bake in the oven in time for the end of the session.

If there is no time to decode the message in the session, give out the codebreaker so that storykeepers can decipher the code in their roll at home.

B5: INVITATIONS (10 MINS)

Make invitations for friends to join The Storykeepers club or to invite people to a special family event. You could make paper invitations by folding a piece of A4 paper into four or card invitations with a single fold. Storykeepers can design their own, especially if you provide the artwork. For further ideas see *Here's one I made earlier*, Kathryn Copsey (SU).

B6: GROUP WORK/ACTIVITY SHEETS (20 MINS)

Three amazing things happened in today's stories about Jesus: the dove came from heaven, Jesus calmed the storm and the wild man. You may need to ask specific questions to jog the memories of the storykeepers. This is another opportunity to build up your relationship with individual children.

5–8s: The children can colour in their pictures at home if time is short.

8–11s: The activity sheet for the 5–8s contains pictures of each of the incidents. You can photocopy and enlarge them for the postcard pictures for use by less confident artists.

Encourage the children to imagine they were there at one of these occasions. How would they have felt? This is an opportunity for them to enter into the reality of a Bible story. Some children will need help to imagine themselves there. You may make a group decision to concentrate on one of the stories. To talk about all of them will lead to a rich discussion but might need firm handling.

The question on everyone's lips was 'Who is Jesus?'. It is obvious he is amazing if he can do wonderful things.

In preparation think how you would describe Jesus. Share your ideas with the children as evidence that you too are learning about Jesus.

5–8s: Prompt the storykeepers with ideas of what may make them afraid, eg the dark, spiders, bigger children.

8–11s: Try to work out together why Jesus was able to do such amazing things. The disciples realised that Jesus has power to change scarey or bad things. He can do the same today. It may help to use the card below to clarify what the storykeepers think of Jesus. Talk with God about situations in life where storykeepers want Jesus to help.

NAME ....

I think that Jesus is/was (tick the box)

a) a good man ☐
b) sent by God ☐
c) a fairy tale ☐
d) I'm not sure ☐

So what I am going to do is

a) find out more about him ☐
b) get to know him better ☐
c) trust him more and more ☐
d) ask him to help me ☐
e) nothing ☐

STILL HUNGRY?

C1: PEN PALS

Why not link up with another group like your own? This could be in the same town, another part of the country or another country. Write to them telling them about your group and what you like about belonging to it. They could write on storykeeper scrolls for greater effect.

In order for this to work, leaders will have to do some hard work in the initial stages. If you are a school group, Scripture Union schools' workers will know about other groups like your own. If you are a church-based group, your church leaders probably know which churches in your area are running holiday or mid-week clubs. If you are a local group then you could meet up at some stage and have a fun day together. Encourage the storykeepers in their 'scroll-writing' to share their favourite stories of Jesus.

C2: FAVOURITE BIBLE BITS

It can be very revealing to find out what others think of the Bible. Make it possible for storykeepers to find out other people's favourite stories of Jesus. They can do this either by asking local people such as parents, teachers or group leaders, or, if you feel adventurous, by writing to ask famous people (include a stamped addresssed envelope!). Make a display of your replies.

C3: PARENTS' COFFEE MORNING

Storykeepers can invite their parents to a special morning. As hosts they make and serve drinks and snacks (eg, iced biscuits, buns). Parents can watch an episode of the video and the children can also tell the stories of Jesus themselves by acting or by using paper bag puppets with narrators and mime. Copies of *The Storykeepers* books and videos can be on sale.

C4: USE THE INTERNET

To develop the theme of different forms of communication, why not use the E-mail or the Internet to contact Christians in another part of the world? Set up in advance, this would be a fantastic resource and could produce immediate results.

C5: QUESTIONNAIRE

Ask as many people as possible what three words they would use to describe Jesus. Children and adults can do this together. It can apply to people inside the church and those who are unchurched. Collate the answers and present them in a newsletter or report back to the church or The Storykeepers club.

FOR ADULTS
C6: MOCKING JESUS

Zak refused to see Jesus mocked. In what ways do we feel that Jesus is taunted in our society? Why should we feel strongly about this? What can we do? Allow for a time of repentance, leading to worship of the risen Jesus.

C7: EVIL IN THE WORLD

Many people outside the church feel strongly about evil in the world, about both natural disasters and those induced by human decision. Use a series of newspaper headlines to identify contempory issues. In the light of this episode of *The Storykeepers*, what does God have to say about evil?

C8: THE ONLY SON

The Scripture Union video *Under the Shadow* contains a documentary on the Bishop of Tehran whose son was killed. He talks about how they coped with that.

RAGING WATERS

Here are three pictures about the stories. Talk together about each one.

Choose one of the stories. Imagine what it would have been like to be there. Draw on these faces how you think you would have felt

What things make you afraid? Write or draw them in the empty box.

  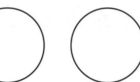

shocked   amazed   frightened

surprised   excited   ——————

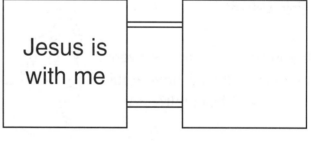

Jesus is with me

Jesus is the Son of God so although things frighten us, he is always with us when we are afraid.

Use this prayer to talk with God:

Dear God, thank you that Jesus is with me when I am afraid. Help me remember that Jesus is the Son of God and that he loves me.

Amen

31

RAGING WATERS

Imagine you were at one of the events in today's stories. Write a postcard to tell your family at home about it all.

When you watch the news what makes you scared? Does anything make you afraid at school? Write about this in the space below.

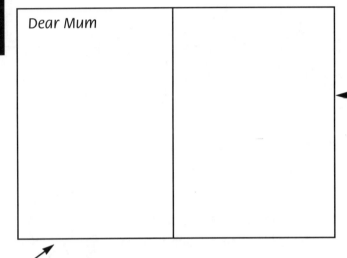

Dear Mum

Stick or draw a picture here

Yours sincerely!
Love and kisses!
Best wishes!

If you had been at the event on your postcard, how would you have felt?

Use the code breaker to discover why Jesus can help us when we are afraid.

A	B	C	D	E	F	G	H	I	J	K	L	M
Z	Y	X	W	V	U	T	S	R	Q	P	O	N

R ZN DRGS BLF ZODZBH

Matthew 28:20

_ _ _   _ _   _ _ _ _   _ _ _   _ _ _ _ _ _

Ring the words which describe how you would feel:

AMAZED

EXCITED

SURPRISED

AFRAID

SAD

SHOCKED

HAPPY

WORRIED

or add your own.

Write a prayer about when you want Jesus to be with you.

Dear God,

_____

_____

_____ Amen.

EPISODE 3

CATACOMB RESCUE

● ● ● ● ● ● ● ● ● ● ● ● ●

AIM

To show that if we accept the words of Jesus, we will behave in ways that will please God. For example, we will love and forgive our enemies or those who are different from us.

THE STORY IN BRIEF

ACT I

On their way to a meeting with other Christians, Ben, Helena and the children are behaving very cautiously. Roman soldiers are looking for Ephraim who is known as the greatest Storykeeper. The Christians arrive at the meeting giving their secret sign. Ephraim, who is there, is introduced. He says that Jesus is the greatest storyteller. He tells **The story of the Good Samaritan**. There is a stranger at the meeting who Zak feels is acting suspiciously.

ACT II

The stranger, Felonius, reports to Nero that Ephraim is in Rome. Nero orders the two centurions, Nihilus and Tacticus, to search the city for him. Justin bumps into some soldiers and hurries back to warn the others. Ephraim is going to Genoa to 'plant seeds' which prompts Ben to tell Helena **The story of the sower**. Justin and Anna escape with Ephraim through the back window, while Stouticus and Nihilus burst in through the front door. Justin, Anna and Ephraim set off for the catacombs. Ben has arranged for the Christians to meet at Zedekiah's cave that night.

ACT III

 As Ben enters the catacombs to meet up with Ephraim, Justin and Anna, Nihilus sees his lantern. He and Tacticus chase after Ben. Bravely Anna tries to bring down the roof of the catacomb, but that separates the children from Ben and Ephraim. Tacticus falls down a hole, but Nihilus refuses to help. The children rescue Tacticus. Anna explains to him that they had to help, just like the Samaritan in the story Jesus told. Meanwhile the Christians are anxious about Justin and Anna. They want revenge on the soldiers. Ephraim talks about forgiveness and tells **The story of the unforgiving servant**. Tacticus appears with the children and says, 'If the people who hear these stories become like these children, then all of Rome should hear about your Jesus.' He gives Ephraim some more travel papers.

BIBLE BASE

The stories in this episode of *The Storykeepers* can be found in the following passages:

Story One	The Good Samaritan	Luke 10:25–37	told by Ephraim
Story Two	The sower	Mark 4:1–12	told by Helena
Story Three	The unforgiving servant	Matthew 18:21–35	told by Ephraim

BEN'S SNACK MENU
(60 MINS)

10 mins	**A1**	Find a partner
10 mins	**A2**	Video: Act I
3 mins	**A3**	*Keep the story alive* song
7 mins	**A4**	Discussion
10 mins	**A5**	Video: Act II
15 mins	**A6**	Group work
5 mins	**A7**	Video: Act III

RECOMMENDED BEN'S THREE COURSE MENU
(2 HOURS)

10.00	**B2**	Make a passport
10.15	**A2**	(Video: Act 1) and **A3**
10.30	**B3**	Make something for someone else
10.45		Refreshments
10.55	**A4** and **A5**	(Video: Act II)
11.10	**B6**	Group work
11.30	**B4**	Pray
11.35	**B5**	Board game
11.50	**A7**	(Video: Act III)

YOU WILL NEED

- *The Storykeepers* video
- Words of the *Keep the story alive* song

A1: List of characteristics for the matching game and a whistle.

A4: A large sheet of paper and pen.

A6: **5-8s** Pens and paper bags; **8–11s** Pictures of famous people.

B1: Pens, pencils and paper.

B2: Blank passport, wax candle, matches, a coin.

B3: Ingredients for making things.

B5: DIY board game as large as possible, counters and dice. You might want to make it larger than the twenty squares in our sample.

B6: One copy of the activity sheet for each child.

BEN'S SNACK MENU

A1 : FIND A PARTNER (10 MINS)

Storykeepers are instructed to run around in the space available. Every now and then, blow a whistle and call out a personal characteristic, for example, hair colour, shoe size, hobbies. Storykeepers have to find a matching partner – someone with the same hair colour/shoe size as themselves – as quickly as possible. Comment that we often feel more drawn towards and make friends with people who are similar to ourselves. In the first of today's stories, we hear about someone who befriends and helps a man who would naturally have been his enemy.

A2: VIDEO ACT I (10 MINS)

End as the soldiers are sent out to search for the Christians.

A3: SONG (3 MINS)

Sing the *Keep the story alive* song.

A4: DISCUSSION (7 MINS)

Make a list on a large sheet of paper of the sort of people storykeepers find hard to like. Avoid being personal, but you could make suggestions such as the newcomer or the bully. In the story a man asked Jesus whom he was supposed to love. Jesus challenged him (and us as well) to love and help people who might not like us, who might even try to harm us. Ben and his friends were learning the lessons of the story – watch how they react to the Roman soldiers.

A5: VIDEO ACT II (10 MINS)

End as Ben's light is spotted going down into the catacombs (a cliffhanger).

A6: GROUP WORK (10 MINS)

5–8s: Use paper bags and draw faces on them. With these bags retell the story of the Good Samaritan. This will reinforce what happened in the story.

8–11s: Children love drama. The story of the Good Samaritan has a large cast of robbers, the injured man, the three passers-by and the innkeeper. Let the children act out the story using mime, then talk about how each of the passers-by felt. Why did the Samaritan stop? In conclusion try to identify those whom the storykeepers find hard to like but who are none the less in need. There are some suggestions in B6 of ways in which drama could be used to think of present-day examples of the parable which relate to a child's experience.

A7: VIDEO: ACT III (5 MINS)

You may want to make time for storykeepers to act out what happened to Anna, Justin, Nihilus and Tacticus. How did all four react? Why did Anna want to help but Justin didn't? Draw out the parallels with the story Jesus told.

BEN'S THREE COURSE MENU

B1: AN IDEAL FRIEND (15 MINS)

Set the children in groups of three or four to draw a cartoon picture of their ideal friend. They can add captions explaining the particular characteristics, for example laughter lines showing a sense of humour, an open ear for someone ready to listen, big hands for helping others. Show some of the pictures to the whole group as the storykeepers explain their ideas. Did any of the descriptions include something about a friend being helpful? We may try to help our friends, but how many of us would be willing to help an enemy?

B2: MAKE A PASSPORT (15 MINS)

Storykeepers can make their own passport. They will need a 'photo' and can write their name, age, likes and dislikes, school and favourite colour. To save time (or to help younger ones) prepare a blank 'form' on card for them to fill in. The passport could be sealed with melted candle wax stamped with a coin.

The passport is today's entry permit to The Catacombs. Group leaders may need to keep these until storykeepers need them.

B3: MAKE SOMETHING FOR SOMEONE ELSE (20 MINS)

Here are some ideas:

● Sweets for an elderly person living alone;
● Pop-up welcome cards for someone who has just moved to the district;
● Paper flowers for someone who is unwell;
● A salt-dough badge;
● Earrings or a fridge magnet for a family member.

Stress that each item is made for *someone else*. Recipes and ideas can be found in *Here's one I made earlier*, Kathryn Copsey (SU).

B4: PRAY (5 MINS)

In groups, everyone stands in a circle with their hands on the shoulders of the person in front. Check that they know this storykeeper's name. All shout out at the same time, 'Lord Jesus, help (N) to love people like you do.' Turn round, face the other way and do the same.

B5: BOARD GAME (15 MINS)

In groups play the board game opposite. The board game could be drawn out to include:

move ahead squares – shared lunch with friend who had forgotten theirs; invited new boy to join my group; offered sweets to everyone in class, including Pamela Smart; partnered class wimp at PE; refused to join the group teasing Lee Kee Tui;

move back or miss a turn squares – swore to get revenge on Jason Black who dropped my book in the mud; wouldn't let my sister play with me; ignored a little boy crying in the playground; bought the last bag of crisps at the Tuck Shop, so Jamie Robinson couldn't get it;

forfeit squares – sit on a balloon and burst it; stand on a chair and count 1–10 backwards; find five things beginning with the letter P; think of four good things that have happened this week; hop backwards across the room.

B6: GROUP WORK – ACTIVITY SHEETS (20 MINS)

Jesus told us to love and help each other and our enemies. For the Storykeepers, living in Rome, that included loving Nero and those Roman soldiers who were out to get them. (Not all Romans were their enemies.) Explore what it means to love and help those with whom storykeepers find they don't naturally get on. Why should we do this? Can you imagine what it was like for the man who was attacked in the story? As the children draw and colour, talk about the story.

What practical things does Jesus want us to do to help people?

5–8s: Talk about how it is not enough to say you'll help – actions are needed too.

8–11s: Storykeepers may ask why Samaritans and Jews were enemies. Jews thought that Samaritans, from the area called Samaria, didn't worship God properly. They weren't proper Jews. A Jewish traveller would go the long way round to avoid having to pass through Samaria. As storykeepers do the wordsearch, talk about what attitudes the Samaritan did and didn't have.

The Samaritan helped someone who was very different from himself, someone who was seen as an enemy. What sort of things can you do to show your love for different sorts of people?

8–11s: You may want to use the suggestions for the drama in **A6** and build on that by acting out present-day scenarios where children have helped the outsider or the enemy. For example:

● In the playground some boys were bullying a younger child. What would you do?
● At lunchtime you noticed a new child sitting on their own. What would you do?
● Jimmy Smith is always teasing you about going to church and making the rest of the class laugh at you. One day on the way home from school, you see him fall off his bike and cut his head. What would you do?

Encourage the children to think of a specific 'outsider' whom they can care for. What makes that a particularly difficult thing to do? Then use the prayer suggestion in **B4**.

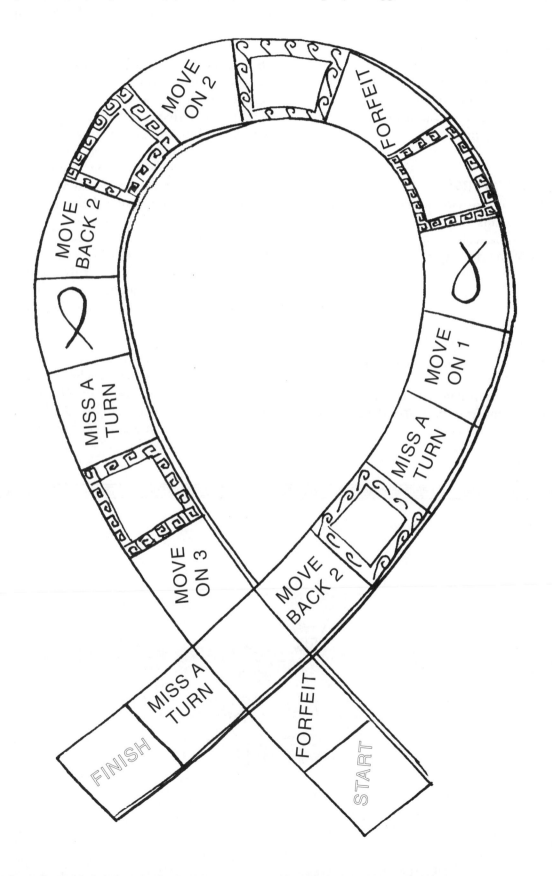

STILL HUNGRY?

C1: SUNFLOWER CITY
The Church Urban Fund are running a scheme where you can grow sunflowers and be sponsored to do it. Half of the proceeds go to them and half to projects of your choice. You can receive a pack from Church Urban Fund, 2 Great Peter Street, London, SW1P 3LX.

C2: SPONSORSHIP PROJECT
Find out about the sponsorship projects run by TEAR Fund, Operation Christmas Child, Christian Aid or CAFOD. Collect money each week to send away and encourage the children to get involved by writing letters.

C3: MEMORY VERSE
'Forgive others, just as God forgave you because of Christ' (Ephesians 4:32b). Write out this verse on rice paper using icing pens. Get the children to eat pieces of the rice paper as the verse is learnt.

FOR ADULTS AND CHILDREN
C4: MODERN PARALLELS
Put yourselves in the place of the children in the story. Would you have helped Tacticus? In groups think of modern equivalents. What prevents us from being or helps us to be a 'Good Samaritan'?

C5: FORGIVENESS
The story of the unforgiving servant is not the focus of the material in this resource, but there are plenty of issues to explore. For example, what is involved in forgiveness, as individuals and also in wider society? There are plenty of contemporary examples of forgiveness and the refusal to forgive, just look in the newspapers over the course of a week.

C6: FURTHER DISCUSSION
Discuss the demands of making a stand for our Christian faith in a hostile environment. You could particularly focus upon life for Christians in a hostile Muslim country in North Africa, where there are many parallels between their life and the storykeepers in Rome AD 64. For further information contact Arab World Ministries, PO Box 51, Loughborough, Leics LE11 0ZQ.

C7: RESEARCH
Find out all you can about life in first century Rome. If you live near a site of Roman interest you could arrange for a trip there. It would have particular interest because of the link with the Storykeepers.

CTVC video *Words into Action* has a programme on love which teaches on the subject of forgiveness. In the series *The RE Collection* (BBC Education) there is an excellent programme on forgiveness which would be a good discussion starter.

CATACOMB RESCUE

Picture the road where the robbers attacked the man. Draw what goes in each box.

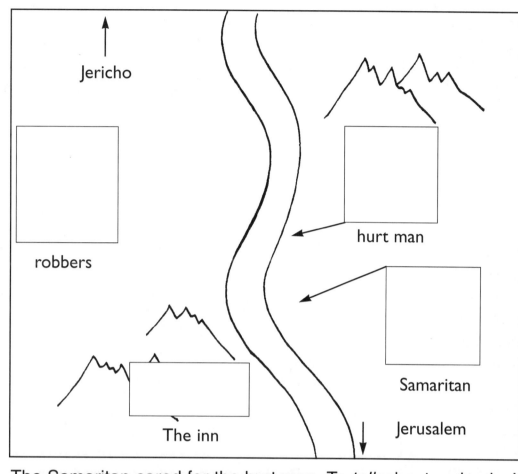

Jericho

robbers

hurt man

Samaritan

The inn

Jerusalem

The Samaritan cared for the hurt man. To *talk* about caring isn't enough. We need to show we care by *doing* something. Join the picture with the right action.

What things can you do to help?

Someone who needs help	How to help

Talk to God as a group. Ask him to *help* us love others as he loves us.

CATACOMB RESCUE

Can you imagine the road where the robbers attacked the traveller? Draw a picture in each box. Where will you put the other two travellers?

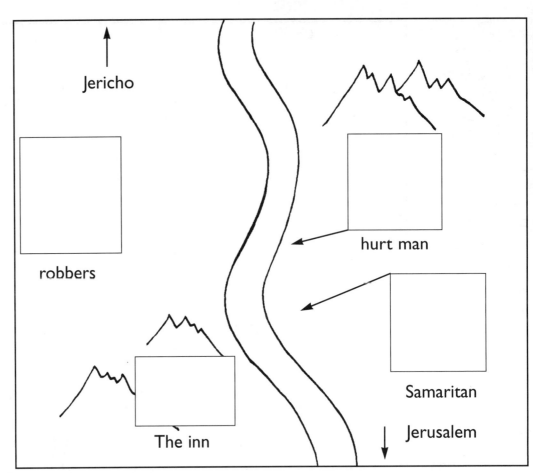

Jericho

robbers

hurt man

Samaritan

The inn

Jerusalem

The Samaritans and the injured man were enemies, but that didn't stop the Samaritan helping his enemy. Find the words in the wordsearch which describe attitudes to other people. There are eleven.

S	P	I	T	E	G	S
E	C	K	I	N	D	E
L	O	V	I	N	G	R
F	O	Y	Z	A	L	V
I	L	N	I	C	G	I
S	Y	L	L	U	B	N
H	E	L	P	I	N	G

Sort the words into the right columns

Please God	Displease God

Think of someone you find it hard to love.

Lord Jesus, please help me to love

_____

in the way that you love me.

EPISODE 4

READY, AIM, FIRE!

. . . .

AIM

To show that just as all the people in the stories of Jesus had to trust him, so we need to trust what Jesus said and believe he can help us. We, like Zak, have to learn that what matters to Jesus is what we're really like, not what we pretend to be.

THE STORY IN BRIEF

ACT 1

Mordecai, a Christian and Zak's uncle, is being chased by soldiers. Zak tries to help him but Mordecai is eventually saved by Ben. Zak is upset because he was keen to show off and prove his worth to Mordecai and has failed. The children ask Mordecai to tell them about his exploits. Zak, trying to be superior, shows he can't be bothered with children. Mordecai's response is to tell them stories about **Jesus' attitude to children**. Meanwhile in Nero's palace, a plan is hatched to set fire to the merchants' district (where tonight's meeting is to be held), in order to clear an area for Nero's building project. Darius slips out to warn Ben.

ACT II

Ben tells a story to encourage the Christians to keep going. He tells **The story of blind Bartimaeus**. At the end of the story Darius arrives with the news of the catapults in place to firebomb the area. The bombing begins. The Christians try putting the fire out. Tacticus manages to limit the effectiveness of the firebombs. The Christians decide to evacuate. While Ben and the others escape on a wagon, Helena tells **The story of Jesus healing the man with the paralysed hand**, to show that doing what is right is most important. Zak, driving the wagon, goes too fast, the horse gets frightened and they head straight for the fire.

ACT III

The runaway wagon is stopped by Ben. They all come to a halt at an intersection with a Roman archer statue. Surrounded by Romans in the hills, Nihilus sees them. There is no way of escape. Zak admits to trying to impress Mordecai. He suddenly has a brainwave. They use the archer statue as a catapult to blast a hole in the aqueduct. Water gushes out and puts out the flames.

BIBLE BASE

The stories in this episode of *The Storykeepers* can be found in the following passages:

Story One	Jesus blesses the children	Mark 9:33–37; 10:13–16	told by Mordecai
Story Two	Blind Bartimaeus	Mark 10:46–52	told by Ben
Story Three	The man with a paralysed hand	Mark 3:1–6	told by Helena

BEN'S SNACK MENU
(60 MINS)

10 mins	**A1**	Video: Act I
4 mins	**A2**	*Keep the story alive* song
7 mins	**A3**	Discussion part I
10 mins	**A4**	Video: Act II
7 mins	**A5**	Discussion part II
7 mins	**A6**	Doing what's right
10 mins	**A7**	Group work
5 mins	**A8**	Video: Act III

RECOMMENDED BEN'S THREE COURSE MENU
(2 HOURS)

10.00	**B4**	Bookmarks
10.10	**A1**	(Video: Act I) and **A2**
10.25	**A3**, **B5**	Mask making or **B2** Games of skill
10.50		Refreshments
11.00	**A4**	(Video: Act II) and **A5**
11.15	**B1**	Obstacle course
11.25	**B7**	Group work
11.45	**A8**	(Video: Act III)

YOU WILL NEED

- The *Storykeepers* video
- Words of the *Keep the story alive* song

A3: Picture of Zak on card or OHP transparency (see page 57).

A7: 5–8s Prepared sheets and pens.

B1: Obstacles, targets and blindfolds for an obstacle course.

B2: Donkey pictures, drawing pins, donkey tails, buckets, table tennis balls, foam footballs, pre-cut holes to aim at, tin cans, bean bags.

B4: Felt-tip pens for colouring, prepared bookmarks, artwork, scissors, glue, and stiff card for making bookmarks.

B5: Rolls of plaster gauze called *Art Roc*, *Vaseline*, swimming caps, a bowl of lukewarm water, pair of scissors or material to make other sorts of masks.

B7: One copy of the activity sheet for each child.

BEN'S SNACK MENU

A1: VIDEO: ACT I (10 MINS)

End as Darius leaves the palace to go and warn Ben.

A2: SONG (3 MINS)

Sing the *Keep the story alive* from page 14.

A3: DISCUSSION – PART I (7 MINS)

Prepare a large cut-out or acetate picture of Zak. What sort of things does Zak do? Write down what the storykeepers tell you and stick their comments onto the picture. We all try and do things to impress people, to pretend that we are different from what we are really like. Ask the storykeepers what sorts of things we do. Add those to the picture too.

A4: VIDEO: ACT II (10 MINS)

End on a cliffhanger as the wagon heads straight for the fire.

A5: DISCUSSION – PART II (5 MINS)

Zak has been trying to do things to impress people but has failed. God isn't impressed by what we do – he sees what we are really like. That's what Jesus was like in today's stories – remind the children of the details of the stories. Everyone else with Jesus may have only seen unimportant children who didn't matter, a poor blind beggar and a man unable to help himself, but they were important to Jesus. How did he show they mattered to him?

Although there may not be anything wrong with us physically, there are always thoughts in our heads and things we do that no one knows about, which need putting right. That was what Zak was struggling with. You may wish to expand on this – Jesus not only showed he cared for people and healed them, he was also able to forgive them for what they had done that displeased God.

A6: DOING WHAT'S RIGHT (7 MINS)

It can be really hard to do the right thing when everyone else is trying to make you do the wrong thing. This is especially hard when you are under pressure, as the children were when Nero bombarded the area where the Christians lived. Briefly retell a true life story of someone who persevered against all the odds. One possible story is that of Corrie Ten Boom and her family who hid Jews in their house during the Second World War. You can find this story in *The Hiding Place*, Corrie Ten Boom (Hodders). Storykeepers may be able to think of examples in their own life when they have had to keep on doing what was right, even though it was hard.

A7 GROUP WORK (10 MINS)

5–8s: People thought children were unimportant in the time of Jesus, but Jesus disagreed. We may not think we are very important but God cares about everything we feel. Give each storykeeper a sheet of paper. At the top write 'God cares for me when I am...' and underneath write 'afraid', 'happy', 'sad', 'excited' and 'left out'. Ask them to draw a picture next to each word. At the bottom, write the verse 'Let the children come to me...', Mark 10:14.

Talk with God to thank him for the things that make us happy and excited. Ask him to help us when we are sad or think we don't matter.

8–11s: How did the Christians escape from Nero? In groups finish the story. Which of the three stories about Jesus from the video did the storykeepers like best?

In twos or threes, ask them to share their best story to encourage each other to be brave when they are having a hard time. Do we face any of the same problems that the children did in the video? Will we be laughed at if we go to the Christian club or to church? How does that make us feel?

Ask God to help us be brave at times like this.

A8: VIDEO: ACT III (5 MINS)

BEN'S THREE COURSE MENU

B1: OBSTACLE COURSE (10 MINS)

Set up an obstacle course and blindfold the participants. One or two storykeepers can try to lead a blindfolded person over the course in two ways, either by taking them by the arm and leading them carefully or standing at a distance and shouting instructions. (If three 'teams' play at once, there will be lots of laughs and absolute mayhem!) Ask the blindfolded storykeepers how it felt. Which way worked best?

Make the connection with blind Bartimaeus – what must it have been like to be blind and why is it best if someone leads a blind person over unfamiliar or dangerous territory? Take great care to avoid mocking blind people.

If you know a blind person, ask them to come in to talk about their disability. If they have a guide dog to bring with them, that will be an added interest.

If others are to hear and understand the stories of Jesus, they will find it easier if we lead them rather than shout at them from a distance.

B2: GAMES OF SKILL (10 MINS)

A series of games, adjusted for different age levels, that involve aiming at a target. The storykeepers can try their hand at a range of them. This should help them identify with Zak's failure and success.

- Pin the tail on the donkey
- Bouncing ping pong balls into buckets
- Footballs into holes
- Bean bags on to tin cans
- Marbles rolled through holes cut in cardboard

Further ideas can be found in *Pick N'mix*, Judith Merrill (SU).

B3: 'ZAK SAYS' (5 MINS)

This game is the same as 'Simon says', except the storykeepers do everything that Zak says. Instructions are only obeyed if, for example, 'Zak says, "Clap your hands" '. 'Clap your hands' should evoke no response!

B4: BOOKMARKS (10 MINS)

For the younger ones prepare a bookmark design with the storykeeper characters on one side and the following verse on the other: 'Love your enemies and pray for anyone who ill-treats you,' Matthew 5:44. For the older ones provide artwork for them to cut and paste their own characters on to the bookmark.

This is today's entry permit for The Catacombs.

B5: MASK MAKING (20 MINS PLUS EXTRA TIME TO PAINT IT)

Zak was hiding behind his mask of efficiency and courage. Inside he was really uncertain of himself and maybe even scared. This activity should follow on from the discussion in A3.

HOW TO MAKE AN ART-ROC MASK

Make masks using *Art-Roc* as below. You will need to prepare the strips in advance.

Instructions

1 Prepare the gauze by cutting it into strips, large and small. Keep it away from water as it begins to set as soon as it is wet. Be careful when picking up pieces.

2 Make sure storykeepers wear something old to protect their clothes.

3 Place a swimming cap on the child's head ensuring all hair is away from face. Sit them comfortably in a chair or let them lie down on the floor.

4 Cover the upper part of their face and the edges of the mask with *Vaseline*. Pay particular attention to eyebrows.

5 Wet each strip individually by dipping it into the water and removing it immediately. Squeeze out any excess water and smooth the strip onto the victim's face. Build up one layer before beginning the next. Do not cover the eyes or nostrils.

6 Wait ten minutes before carefully removing the mask. Make holes for string on either side of the mask with a sharp point. Trim the edges to neaten the mask. A child could add some small strips of plaster to tidy the eye holes. Leave it to dry.

You will need to allocate space later in the programme to decorate the mask, either on a future day or later on in the session.

7 The children can draw their design for the mask on paper, planning the outline and colours. By the time they have finished, the mask should be ready to paint. Transfer the design outline on to the mask with a pencil first.

8 Pour out small amounts of paint into pots. Insist children rinse their brushes before using the next colour.

You may want to make other sorts of masks. For example, use card or papier mâché on a balloon. The latter will take more than one day to dry.

B6: THE BIBLE IN BRAILLE (10 MINS)

Arrange for someone who is blind, is a Christian and reads Braille to come to talk with the storykeepers about reading the Bible in Braille. It would be ideal if they could bring one of the stories from today's video in Braille for the children to touch. Talk about what it is like to have to trust others when you are blind. You may want to lead the discussion on to what it means to trust Jesus.

B7: GROUP WORK/ACTIVITY SHEETS (20 MINS)

 In each story Jesus helped people who could not help themselves and who needed to trust Jesus to care for them. By this session many storykeepers will trust you and feel comfortable with you. Build on that trust as you talk about the need to trust in Jesus and how this is possible. Boasting and acting like a big-head suggests that someone is OK, but inside this is usually far from the truth. Was Zak really happy inside? Make time at the end for any child who wants to talk further.

In both groups help the children to spot the differences.

 Each of the people Jesus helped had to be willing to trust him.
5–8s: Imagine what it felt like to be one of the people from today's stories. Allow the storykeepers to talk about their feelings.
8–11s: Encourage storykeepers to talk about what they find difficult, such as moving house or school, a family break-up, jealousy, unfair treatment, bullying. When we are faced with hard things we can easily try to impress others, like Zak did, to hide how we feel.

What stops us from being brave?
5–8s: When we face difficult situations we need to be brave and to trust Jesus. Identify situations that relate to the children where they need to be brave. Ask Jesus to help them to be brave. Remind storykeepers of the verse on the bookmark.
8–11s: What things stop us telling others about the stories of Jesus? Storykeepers don't just keep the stories to themselves – they want to share them but not everyone wants to hear them. Can storykeepers remember what Tacticus said at the end of Epsiode 3? (See 'The story in brief'.) He is an example of someone who wants to hear more. This is an opportunity to explain that once Jesus had gone back to heaven, God sent his Holy Spirit in place of Jesus. He helps us to know God, to know how to please God, to talk with him and to share the stories of Jesus with others.

SAMPLE BOOKMARK TEMPLATE

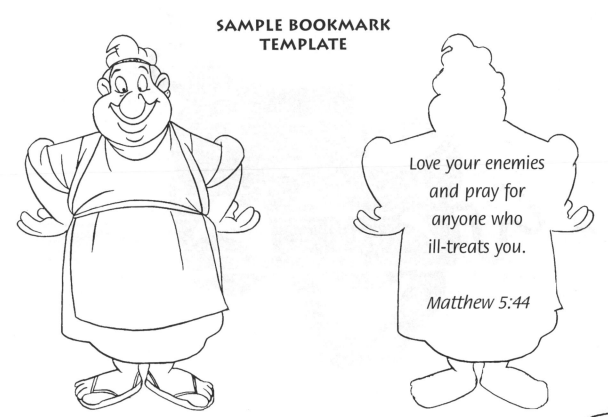

Love your enemies and pray for anyone who ill-treats you.

Matthew 5:44

STILL HUNGRY?

C1: A RESIDENTIAL HOME

Make a link with a residential home for the elderly or disabled. On special occasions like harvest, Christmas and Easter, storykeepers of all ages can visit. Each time they go, the children could sing and tell one of the stories of Jesus. Building long-term relationships can be really important.

C2: NIKOLAI

This is a video about the story of a young boy who needed to be brave in the face of persecution in being a Christian in Eastern Europe under communism. The video lasts about thirty-five minutes. Available from SP/Valley (VC 135).

C3: MAKE A TAPE FOR A BLIND PERSON

Record one of this episode's Bible stories onto tape, using a different voice for each character. This can then be given to a blind person, or you may want to read on to a cassette the whole of this episode, *Catacomb Rescue*. The books are at two reading levels, available from Cassell (see page 64 for details).

FOR ADULTS AND CHILDREN
C4: HIDING BEHIND MASKS

Explore the basis that we have for self-esteem. How much do we genuinely rely on God and how much on our background, natural gifting and contacts? What masks do we wear? How much do we hide behind our masks? What does God have to say about that? The video *In the bin* (SU) focusses upon the masks we hide behind in front of other people and in front of God.

C5: MASK MAKING

Why not spend an activity day making masks of various types, which could include the ones featured in **B5**? Your local library should have several books about mask making. Face-painting could be another option. This could be combined with a showing of this episode of *The Storykeepers*.

READY, AIM, FIRE!

Can you spot the eight differences?

Who were the people who were with Jesus in today's stories? If you were them, what would you have felt like? Colour the words that make you feel safe.

Here are some times where we find it hard to trust Jesus. Tick the box if any of them has happened to you.

HAPPY	**SCARED**
SAFE	**AFRAID**
LONELY	**UNCERTAIN**

Talk to Jesus about the things you find difficult. Ask him to help you trust him.

Draw yourself

47

READY, AIM, FIRE!

Can you spot the eight differences?

Ben said, "One thing's for certain. They won't be able to keep us quiet for ever." Storykeepers want to share the stories of Jesus, but people don't always want to listen. Think of what some people say about Jesus.

They say…

What difficult things did the Storykeepers have to face in Rome in AD **64**? What hard things are there in your life?

Discover how Jesus has promised to help us tell others about him. Start at the arrow and write down every third letter.
Acts 1:8

Storykeepers AD **64**	Storykeepers now

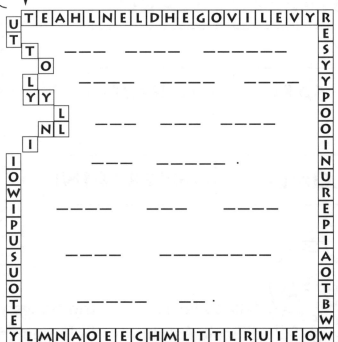

Talk to God. Thank him for his Holy Spirit. Ask him to help you tell others about Jesus.

EPISODE 5

CAPTURED!

· · · · · · · · · · · · · ·

AIM

To show that even though we have turned our back on God, he is willing to welcome us if we choose to ask for his forgiveness.

THE STORY IN BRIEF

ACT I

The children are preparing the granary for a meeting. Cyrus remembers performing with his father. Zak arrives breathless, seeking revenge on the Romans. Ben tells **The story of the Centurion's servant** to show that not all Roman soldiers are bad. The soldiers arrive and a chase ensues. Cyrus is caught. A Roman senator, Flavius, seeing his acrobatics, buys him from the soldiers. Flavius takes him away.

ACT II

Anna has noticed the crest on Flavius' carriage which enables Ben to identify who he is. At Flavius' estate, Cyrus thinks he is going to be ill-treated and tries to escape. But Flavius dresses him up and feeds him well. He plans to use Cyrus' juggling skills to impress Senator Pithius and sway his vote in the senate. He even gives Cyrus a new name: 'Cyroo – Prince of Jugglers'. The others plan to rescue Cyrus. They travel towards Flavius' estate. Ben tells part one of **The story of the lost son** (up to the point where he finds the job of feeding the pigs). When they arrive at Flavius' house, Cyrus doesn't want to be rescued so they leave without him.

ACT III

Flavius's banquet works a treat, but later that night his slaves revolt, burning the fields and warehouses and stealing Flavius's possessions. Flavius tries to blame Cyrus who runs away. Later that night news reaches Ben who decides to find Cyrus. Justin wonders why they should bother. Helena defends Cyrus and tells part two of **The story of the lost son**, stressing the point that it was difficult for the son to come back and difficult for the older brother to welcome him too. They find Cyrus and Justin welcomes him by giving Cyrus his cloak.

BIBLE BASE

The stories in this episode of *The Storykeepers* can be found in the following passages:

Story One	The Centurion's servant	Luke 7:1–10	told by Helena
Story Two	The lost son	Luke 15:11–32	told by Helena

BEN'S SNACK MENU
(60 MINS)

5 mins	**A1**	Game
10 mins	**A2**	Video: Act I
4 mins	**A3**	Song
10 mins	**A4**	Video: Act II
7 mins	**A5**	Choices
10 mins	**A6**	Group work
5 mins	**A7**	Video: Act III
5 mins	**A8**	Conclusion

RECOMMENDED BEN'S THREE COURSE MENU
(2 HOURS)

10.00	**B4**	Secret Password
10.10	**A2/A4**	(Video: Acts I and II) and **A3**
10.35	**B1**	Circus skills or **B2** Party food
10.55		Refreshments
11.05	**A7**	(Video: Act III)
11.15	**B6**	Group work
11.35		Party time
11.50	**A3**	and **B3** Reading the stories yourself

YOU WILL NEED

- The *Storykeepers* video
- Words for the *Keep the story alive* song

A5 : Shop labels for the corners of the room.

B1 : Juggling balls, teach yourself juggling video, plastic plant pots, string, face paints.

B2 : Biscuits, icing sugar, jam, frozen pastry, *Quik-jel*, fruit, chocolate, bread, tuna fish, cream cheese, margarine, food colouring.

B3 : *The Storykeepers* books, starter copies of *Let's Go* and *Check it Out!*.

B4 : The following message written in code, using one of the codes from Episode 2, **A3**: 'Storykeepers keep alive the stories of Jesus'.

This is for older storykeepers and can be written around the fish shape that the Storykeepers used as their secret sign. For younger children, draw the fish sign in candle wax on a piece of paper. Storykeepers can paint over the fish to discover the secret sign. You will need to find somewhere to put these to dry.

B5 : Pens and paper or small notebooks for writing a diary.

B6 : One copy of the activity sheet for each child. You may want to read the story of the runaway son in Luke 15:11–32. If so, make sure you have enough Bibles.

BEN'S SNACK MENU

A1: GAME (5 MINS)

Two leaders can either act out the following humorous roles or let the storykeepers do the acting. The audience has to decide whom they would trust in the following circumstances.

● You want to cross a busy road. Who will you trust to help you: a policeman/woman or someone with lots of luggage and no free hands?
● You need help for a bad leg. Who will you trust to help you: a doctor/nurse or someone who is obviously very sick themselves?
● You want a ride in a bus. Whom will you trust to drive you: a bus driver (with uniform) or someone with an L plate?

Was it hard to decide whom to trust? How did you decide? That's what Cyrus had to think about in 'Captured!'.

A2: VIDEO: ACT I (10 MINS)

End as Cyrus is dragged away.

A3: SONG (4 MINS)

Sing the *Keep the story alive* song.

A4: VIDEO ACT II (10 MINS)

End as Ben and the rest leave without Cyrus.

A5: CHOICES (7 MINS)

Play an elimination game based on choices. Imagine you are shopping. Label corners of the room as 'baker', 'greengrocer', 'butcher' and 'newsagent'. Call out something you could buy in one of the shops. The storykeepers run to the right shop – last one there is out. Try to fool them by pointing in the wrong direction. Explain that sometimes we make choices which are the wrong ones and sometimes that means we suffer as a result. Just think about the choices Cyrus made.

A6: GROUP WORK (10 MINS)

This is the last session of The Storykeepers. Use it to strengthen relationships, but also to leave the children with a challenge: what choices are they going to make? Are they going to get to know Jesus better and share his stories with others?

5–11s: How do you think the other children felt when Cyrus wouldn't come back with them? What sort of things do other people do to us that make us feel that way? Explain that that is exactly how God feels when we refuse to do what pleases him and when we pretend that he isn't worth bothering with or when we think he just doesn't matter. The great news is that he wants to forgive us and will accept us if we are sorry and are willing to change. Explain that you are going to pray a prayer asking for forgiveness. Any storykeeper can pray it in their heads too. Ask them to let you know if they have. The words of a prayer you could use are in B6.

A7: VIDEO: ACT III (5 MINS)

A8: CONCLUSION (5 MINS)

Explain that just as Cyrus was welcomed back, so God will accept us if we want him to.

BEN'S THREE COURSE MENU

B1: CIRCUS SKILLS (15 MINS)

Cyrus demonstrates his juggling skills and performs in front of Flavius. Provide a range of possible skills to try out:

● Juggling. You will need about fifty bean bags and someone who can do a basic three-ball juggle to teach the storykeepers. Set up a competition to see who can improve the most.

● Stilts. Use plastic plant pots and strong string to make small stilts. Run some races.

● Face painting. Paint clowns' faces or characters from *The Storykeepers* on to the children (someone is bound to want to be Nero!). The children may wish to paint themselves.

B2: PARTY FOOD (15 MINS)

At the end of today's episode Cyrus will return home. Tell the storykeepers that we are going to have a party, but don't tell them why. Enlist their help in making party snacks:

● Iced biscuits;
● Party buns – bake in advance and ice them in the session;
● Jam tarts – buy ready made frozen pastry;
● *Quik-jel* (if you have access to a fridge). Put fruit in the bottom;
● Dip cut-up fruits in melted chocolate;
● Make tuna/cream cheese sandwiches cut into small triangles.

Further ideas for food can be found in *Here's one I made earlier*, Kathryn Copsey (SU). Buy some food colouring and cheap lemonade and have lots of different coloured drinks. You could also make table decorations, place mats and decorate balloons. At the end, make time to enjoy the fruits of your labours – there was a celebration when the son returned home.

B3: READING THE STORIES YOURSELF (10 MINS)

Use copies of the starter versions of *Let's Go* and *Check it Out!* based on Mark's Gospel or Luke's Gospel, and go through them with the storykeepers. The Luke starter contains the story of the lost son and Zacchaeus. The Mark starter includes the stories about when Jesus welcomed a child and when he walked on the water. Give them away along with information about how to regularly receive Scripture Union's current Bible reading material. Copies of *The Storykeepers*

books could be available for children and parents to buy.

B4: SECRET PASSWORD (10 MINS)

Write out the phrase 'Storykeepers keep alive the stories of Jesus' in code for older storykeepers to decipher. Provide them with the codebreaker when they arrive. Draw a fish shape in wax on a piece of paper for younger storykeepers to paint over.

A	B	C	D	E	F	G	H	I	J	K	L	M
z	y	x	w	v	u	t	s	r	q	p	o	n

N	O	P	Q	R	S	T	U	V	W	X	Y	Z
m	l	k	j	i	h	g	f	e	d	c	b	a

This is today's entry permit to The Catacombs.

B5: LOST SON'S DIARY/CYRUS' DIARY (15 MINS)

Storykeepers can write a diary for the lost son or for Cyrus from the story. Prepare pages for them to write or draw their entries. Some storykeepers may want to read or show this to the others. If you have a portable computer, storykeepers could use this.

B6: GROUP WORK/ACTIVITY SHEETS (20 MINS)

Focus on the events in the story of the lost son and the parallel of Cyrus leaving his friends. Make sure both age groups have grasped the story.

With 8–11s you may want to read the story in the Bible in Luke 15:11–32. Ask a good reader to read the story. Others could read the words of the son, the older son and the father.

Children have a genuine fear of getting physically lost but also of being left out and not accepted. Some children in your group may find it hard to believe that God will accept them if they come to him. Think about how you can reassure them of God's love and acceptance. They will easily identify with Cyrus. Make time for the children to respond without putting pressure on them. In your preparation think how you will explain how someone can become a friend of Jesus.

Help storykeepers in both age groups to see how we are all like the lost son in the story and how God is like the father.

What about us?
5–8s: What will we choose to do: be friends of Jesus or not? Use the prayer on the activity sheet as appropriate.

8–11s: In what ways are we like Cyrus and the lost son?

If you are having a party to conclude the holiday club, make sure that you have allowed some space for any questions children may ask or for those who want to tell you what choices they may have made.

For both groups you may want to use the following prayer – photocopy a few copies for children who are ready to say it.

> Dear Jesus,
> ● Thank you that you want me to be your friend.
> ● Thank you that God is like the Father in the story. He can forgive me and welcome me.
> ● I am sorry that I have done things that displease God.
> ● Please forgive me and accept me as your friend.
> Amen.

On pages 61 and 62 there are photocopiable leaflets (one for each age group) to give to any child who has prayed this prayer.

Remember that some storykeepers will already be a friend of Jesus. For others this will still be very new. Be sensitive in how you encourage storykeepers to respond and use this prayer.

GREAT WAYS TO READ THE BIBLE

It's important to find out what the Bible says – and it can be fun too with **Let's Go** and *Check it Out!*

Let's Go is for you if you're 7 or 8. Explore the Bible with Boff the Prof, Jack, Tara, Walls and Ratty. There are lots of things to do each week based on a story from the Bible, like prayers, craft ideas, experiments and quizzes.
There are 4 issues of Let's Go every year – each one costs £2.85.

If you're between 9 and 11 try *Check it Out!* New pages every issue to tear out and file in a funfax binder. Puzzles, prayer ideas, true stories and daily Bible readings help you learn more about God.
Check it Out! costs £2.85 for 3 months' worth of pages.

Both **Let's Go** and *Check it Out!* are available from your local Christian bookshop. If there isn't one near where you live, you can get it direct from Scripture Union at
PO Box 764, Oxford OX4 5FJ.
Tel: 01865 716880.

STILL HUNGRY?

C1: FAMILY FUN EVENT

Organise a family fun event based on *The Storykeepers* theme. There can be refreshments served at the bakery, competitions in the arena (three-legged races, parent and child events, egg and spoon) and lots of stalls in the market place with things to try. Base it around one episode of *The Storykeepers*. As well as letting the video tell the stories of Jesus, enable the children to tell the relevant stories. Younger ones can use puppets and act out the parts; older ones can use drama, sound effects and anything else they have made or used in *The Storykeepers*.

C2: *THE STORYKEEPERS* SERVICE

Organise a special family service in which the children take part. Sing the *Keep the story alive* song with input on the chance to meet Jesus, the greatest storyteller ever. Have available some modern versions of the gospels to buy and children's follow-up material, including SU's Bible reading material for adults and children. Also have available copies of *The Storykeepers* reading, activity and colouring books published by Cassell.

FOR ADULTS AND CHILDREN
C3: RECONCILIATION

Explore the importance of reconciliation between us and God and between us and one another. What did it cost Ben and the father to accept the errant boy? Why is reconciliation such a key issue in our society? *Under the Shadow* (SU) contains documentary material about two people from opposite sides of the divide in Northern Ireland. It comes with discussion material.

C4: THE STORY GOES ON

There are eight more episodes of *The Storykeepers*, distributed by SP/Valley, which are available from your local Christian bookshop or other video outlets. Why not buy another video and use that as a reunion for storykeepers a few weeks after the holiday club? Parents could be invited to discover with their children how the story has gone on! You could use activities which you had no time for in this resource book or let the video suggest other possibilities. The *Keep the story alive* song will be relevant to every episode!

PLANNING THE FINAL EVENT OF THE HOLIDAY CLUB

WHAT IS THIS EVENT?
IT COULD BE ANY OF THESE:

1 *A final session of the holiday club, aimed primarily at the storykeepers.*
You could show another episode in *The Storykeepers* series and develop one of those themes. Show an episode again from early in the week. You would need to introduce the characters and give a flavour of what has been going on all week. (If your service is an hour long, almost half the time would be spent in showing the video.)

2 *An exhibition by the storykeepers of what has been going on all week, aimed primarily at the parents/friends of storykeepers.*
You might want to show clips of a video, sing the song, give an opportunity for children to show the dramas they worked on in episode 4, talk about and show the crafts they made or, discuss one of the themes of the video you have shown. You could reintroduce the message baked in a roll from episode 2, but use another message. Involve as many children as possible but don't spend lots of time in the previous day's session

preparing for this service which could distract from the key theme of that episode.

3 *The beginning of the next stage of building relationships, containing an evangelistic emphasis and an invitation to come back again, aimed at parents and children.*
Look through the ideas suggested in **STILL HUNGRY?** You may want to separate children and adults for part of the service to explore one of these ideas. You could depart from the 'normal' structure of a church service and have an activity event, involving adults and children together. It is important that the occasion is welcoming for the fringe/unchurched adults and that it is clear what is the next event/stage in the relationship building process, with a suitable invitation. For example, if you are planning a Storykeepers midweek club, have ready the details of this and any plans for the next adult event.

Serve refreshments to give a chance to talk with parents and say goodbye to storykeepers. They could have a 'Storykeeper' flavour such as Roman shield biscuits or 'poisoned' buns! This is also the time to have a bookstall which includes *The Storykeepers* books and Bible reading materials.

CAPTURED!

The son who ran away is trying to find his way home. Can you show him the right way? Using a finger from each hand, can you join the father and son?

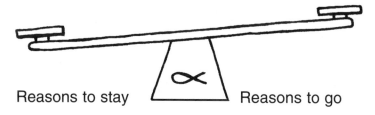

Reasons to stay   Reasons to go

Why does Cyrus choose to stay with Flavius and not go home with Ben?

Cut out the blocks and stick them on the see-saw. Which side is heavier?

MONEY	CLOTHES	FAME

TRUST	FAMILY	OTHER	COMFORT	LOVE	FRIENDS

You can choose whether or not you want to be a friend of Jesus. Talk together about what it means to be a friend of Jesus

55

CAPTURED!

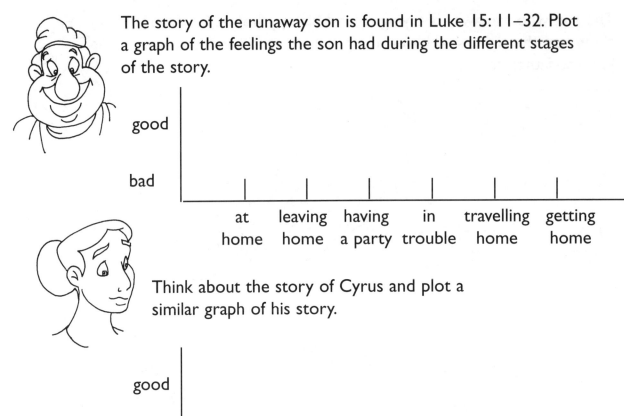

The story of the runaway son is found in Luke 15: 11–32. Plot a graph of the feelings the son had during the different stages of the story.

good

bad

| at home | leaving home | having a party | in trouble | travelling home | getting home |

Think about the story of Cyrus and plot a similar graph of his story.

good

bad

Think about the ways we are like Cyrus, the runaway son.

Cross out every third letter in the sentence below.

IF AWEB COCNFDESSS ODURG SIHNSO TOB GOSD, HLE CRANS ALRWATYS ZBE XTRYUSDTERD TLO FRORSGINVE TUS BANTD TKAKLE OZURZ SITNS BAWBAY.

1 John 1:9

You can choose to trust God to forgive you for the wrong you have done. What will you choose? Talk together about what it means to be forgiven and become a friend of Jesus.

BEN

HELENA

CYRUS

ANNA

JUSTIN

MARCUS

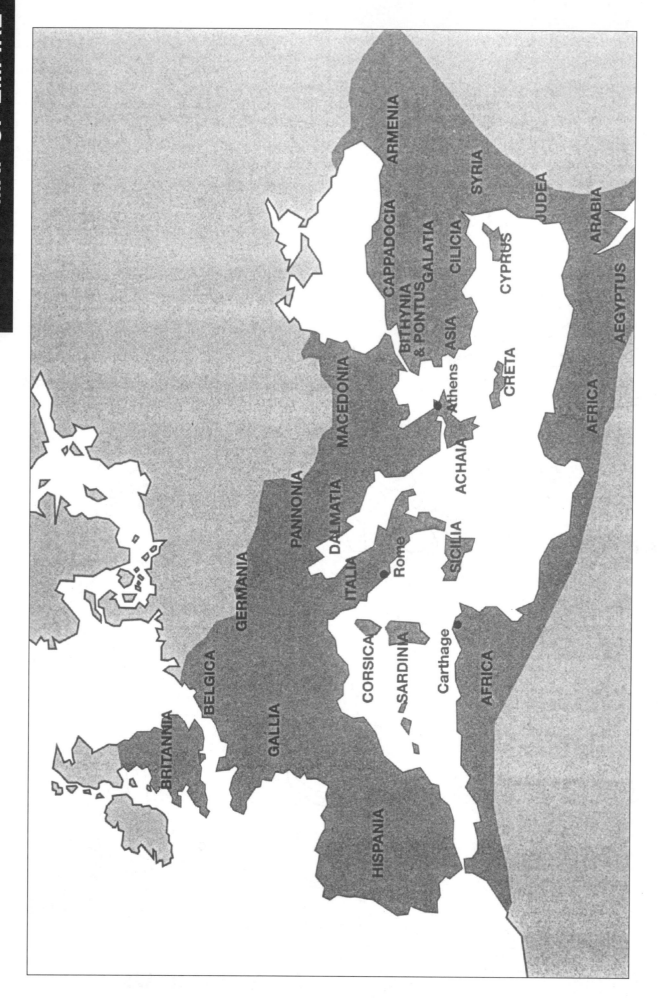

ORGANISING FOLLOW-UP EVENTS FOR ADULTS AND CHILDREN

If our communication of the gospel to children is to be effective it needs to be reflected in a long-term commitment. This is especially true if we are working with children who are second or third generation non-churchgoers. Inevitably this means planning how to work with them on a regular basis. Children are part of a wider community. Our society is no longer simple to categorise. Children will come reflecting a wide mix of cultures. The experience of family will be very mixed too. In some homes family will still carry tremendous importance whilst in others it will be the cause of considerable pain. Even the word 'family' conjures up a range of images: extended families, single parent families, absent parents due to bereavement, work or divorce. Society is also increasingly mobile. It is into this varied and potentially unstable situation that we seek to bring the good news of the gospel. For many children the contact we have with them will be part of a whirlwind of cultural exchanges. This heightens the value of building relationships.

Effective follow-up is vital if we are to see the extension of God's kingdom. We want to welcome children to be part of the faith community of the church. However, they are only likely to trust us and take this step if we have built relationships of trust with them. The starting point for follow-up is the quality and consistency of the individual relationships that we build with the children we contact.

INDIVIDUAL FOLLOW-UP

In theory this is easy to achieve as it simply involves keeping in touch. However, so often much of our effort goes into running events and we miss these vital opportunities. Regular sustained contact is likely to be much more significant then a lot of effort in a short amount of time.

SUGGESTIONS

1) Writing

Children love receiving letters. Writing to them can be a great way to build on a relationship. Remember to treat the letter as an open one that might be read by anyone in the house. Think, 'What would I think as a parent if I read these words?' Avoid using Christian jargon and be simple, honest and personal. Talk about the enjoyment of the time at Storykeepers. Ask them non-threatening questions to which they can give straightforward answers.

2) Special occasions

A card at Christmas, Easter or on birthdays can be of great significance and it shows a personal touch that children and adults will appreciate.

3) Involvement in local schools

If you visited local schools to advertise The Storykeepers you could build stronger links with the school by visiting on a regular basis. There are opportunities for involvement in collective worship. You could offer to listen to children read or help out with school trips. For further ideas look at the leaflet 'Is your church ready for school?', available free from Scripture Union In Schools, 207–209 Queensway, Bletchley, Milton Keynes, MK2 2EB.

4) Libraries

Your church may run a video/book library. If so it makes sense to have *The Storykeepers* videos and books available. Alternatively you may be able to make a gift of the videos and books to the local public library.

ONE-OFF EVENTS

In order to build on this individual contact, you might consider running some one-off follow-up events. Keeping in touch with children would make inviting them to this far easier and more natural. Think about events to which the whole family can come in order to build trust with parents. Be careful to structure the events in a way that includes the children who come on their own.

1) Family fun days

The best model for these events is the School Fair approach. A whole afternoon given over to this would be a great way of involving all the family. Arrange a central arena with a running programme of events and a series of side stalls. Many of the ideas in this book could be used. There could be two occasions when everyone stops to watch *The Storykeepers* video. And if you're outdoors, why not hire a marquee?!

2) Storykeepers Roman Sports

A family sports event on a Roman theme would be another way of involving the whole family in a great day out. Use your imagination to look at fun ways of doing this: Chariot Races, Relays, Throwing the Jelly, Seven-Legged Races etc. Make some Roman costumes and have someone act as the Games opener. You could always award chocolate medals for the winners!

REGULAR EVENTS

1) Weekly clubs

Starting a Storykeepers club would be an excellent way to follow up a special week. For familiarity have a regular routine with familiar songs and use *The Storykeepers* video. Remember that children are less worried by repetition than adults. Since each episode of the video has more than one theme it is possible to re-visit the same episode from a completely different perspective. There are eight more videos available in the series.

2) Monthly celebrations

A regular club may be inappropriate but you might feel able to organise a special event on a once a month basis. To develop relationships the same team of leaders will need to be involved. An extended time together could be very effective, in a 'Kids' praise party' style. If you intend to use this style then it is really important that you have music of high quality and that the event is led by someone with gifts in up-front communication. A video projector and large screen would give *The Storykeepers* stories the best coverage.

THINGS TO CONSIDER

1) Venue

It is very easy to base our approach on a 'come to us' basis. Consider using a 'neutral' venue rather than church premises. Community centres or schools can be good places for working regularly with children. Leisure centres or sports clubs are user-friendly for events where adults and children are together.

2) Organisation

It is really important that the children meet familiar faces at any follow-up events. Make sure that as many as possible of those whom the children have learnt to trust during *The Storykeepers* are available. If this is to be a regular event, children are more likely to return if they get to know the people who run it every week. They like familiarity and routine, so try to have some items that appear every week.

Timing

Think carefully about the most appropriate time for events. If children are to come regularly you will need to meet at a time that is convenient for them and their parents. Try to avoid mealtimes. Be aware that for many Sunday is no longer a special day, so think about a regular event straight after school or in the early evening. When planning events for the whole family, remember that in many homes Saturday is most likely to be the day for leisure activities, but bear in mind other activities occur on that day too, eg football matches, regular shopping. To make a longer event attractive to all, it is important to have parts of the programme all together and parts in which adults and children are separate.

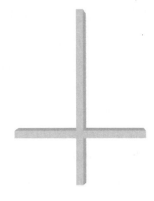

So how can we become God's friends?

1 Thank God for what Jesus did for us.

2 Say sorry for the wrong things we have done.

3 Ask God to forgive us and accept us.

4

All along people had wondered, "Who is Jesus?" He said he was God's son. He told people he had to die so that everyone could become God's friends. He died so that the wrong things we do could be forgiven.

3

PRAYER

Thank you that Jesus died for me. I'm sorry for the wrong things I do. Thank you that you can forgive me. I want to be your friend. Amen

Not everyone liked what Jesus did. The Jewish leaders tried to stop him.

They plotted against Jesus and he was killed. He died on a wooden cross with two thieves — one on each side.

2

The STORY KEEPERS

1

The storykeepers were helped by telling each other the stories of Jesus. We can do that today as well. Do you know the story of how Jesus died?

Turn over to read about it.

The STORY KEEPERS

In the middle of difficult times, we can remind ourselves of the stories of Jesus. That really helps us.

But what really helps us is to realise who Jesus is. The stories are amazing.

But there is something even more amazing.

We can meet him today!

IT'S AMAZING

2

JESUS' BIRTH

His birth was amazing! Angels announced that he had been born. He was visited by people as different as poor shepherds and rich wise men. God's Saviour had been born.

JESUS' WORDS

His words were amazing! People loved Jesus' stories and crowds rushed to hear him. He told them how they ought to live. He also told them he was God come to live among them.

3

JESUS' ACTIONS

He did amazing things. Sick people got better, blind people could see, he calmed a storm and walked on water. These all happened so that people could see that he was God. People knew he loved them.

JESUS' DEATH

His death was amazing! He died on a cross. Although he was not guilty he was killed by the leaders. In his death he was punished for all the wrong things anyone has ever done. God made it possible for us to become his friends.

That wasn't the end. He came back to life so that he could be with us today.

4

WHAT ABOUT YOU?

Because Jesus died and came back to life we don't have to be God's enemies any more. We can become his friends. All we have to do is ask him to forgive us and accept us. If you want to do that, pray the prayer below.

Dear God,
Thank you that Jesus came to earth to show us how to live. Thank you that he died to make it possible for me to be forgiven. I'm sorry for the wrong things I have done. I want to be your friend. Thank you that Jesus is alive today so he can be with me. Help me to listen to you and obey you every day.
Amen.

AMPLE LETTER TO PARENTS WITH A REGISTRATION FORM

: This could be folded in half across the middle, with the logo photocopied on the outside.)

Storykeepers live in Rome in AD 64. Emperor Nero wants to get rid of them. They have the job of keeping alive the stories of Jesus so they are not going to give in to him. But life is full of danger and adventure!

This is YOUR INVITATION to find out more about THE STORYKEEPERS.

Church logo and address
Contact phone number
Date

Dear Parent/Guardian

Would you like your child to discover the adventures of life in Rome in AD 64, when the emperor is after your blood? That's what confronts the Storykeepers, as they keep alive the stories of Jesus, sharing them with others. Why not let your child come along to The Storykeepers, at (details of venue) every morning (or afternoon) from .... to ....?

The Storykeepers is for 5–11 year olds (Reception to Year 6) and is being organised by members of .... (your church), completely free of charge (or state here what the charges are and what they cover, eg refreshments, hire of the hall). There will be a chance to view episodes from *The Storykeepers*, which has been shown on ITV, as well as plenty of fast-moving activity, games, puzzles and adventure. Children themselves will become storykeepers, sharing in the stories of Jesus.

If you would like your child to join The Storykeepers, please complete the registration form below and return it by (date) at the latest. Space is limited so places may have to be allocated on a first-come-first-served basis. Further information will be sent out nearer the time. If you have any queries, please contact (name) on (phone number).

We are looking forward to seeing your child at The Storykeepers.

Your name

The Storykeepers Coordinator

Registration form for The Storykeepers (One per child, please)

Please tear off along the dotted line and return to . . . .

. . . .

. . . . (name and address of coordinator)

Full name of child . . . . Male/Female

Address . . . .

Telephone number . . . . Date of birth . . . . Age on (date of first day) . . . . .

School . . . . Class . . . .

Signature of parent/guardian . . . . Date . . . .